Cooperative Federalism in Employment Security: The Interstate Conference

David G. Williams
West Virginia University

Ann Arbor
Institute of Labor and Industrial Relations
The University of Michigan-Wayne State University
1974

Cooperative Federalism in Employment Security:
The Interstate Conference
Copyright 1974 by The Institute of Labor and
Industrial Relations, The University of Michigan--
Wayne State University. All rights reserved.
Library of Congress Catalog Card No.: 74-620188
ISBN: 0-87736-323-4
Printed in the United States of America

Contents

	Foreword, Daniel H. Kruger	vii
	Preface	xiii
1	The Federal-State Relationship in Employment Security	1
2	Origin and Organization of the Interstate Conference	27
3	Activities and Function of the Interstate Conference	51
4	Influence Relationships and ICESA Impact	77
5	The Role of the ICESA: Operation and Evaluation	91
6	Intergovernmental Relations in Employment Security	113
	Bibliography	133

Figure 1 Organization Of The Manpower Administration,
U. S. Department Of Labor, April 1971

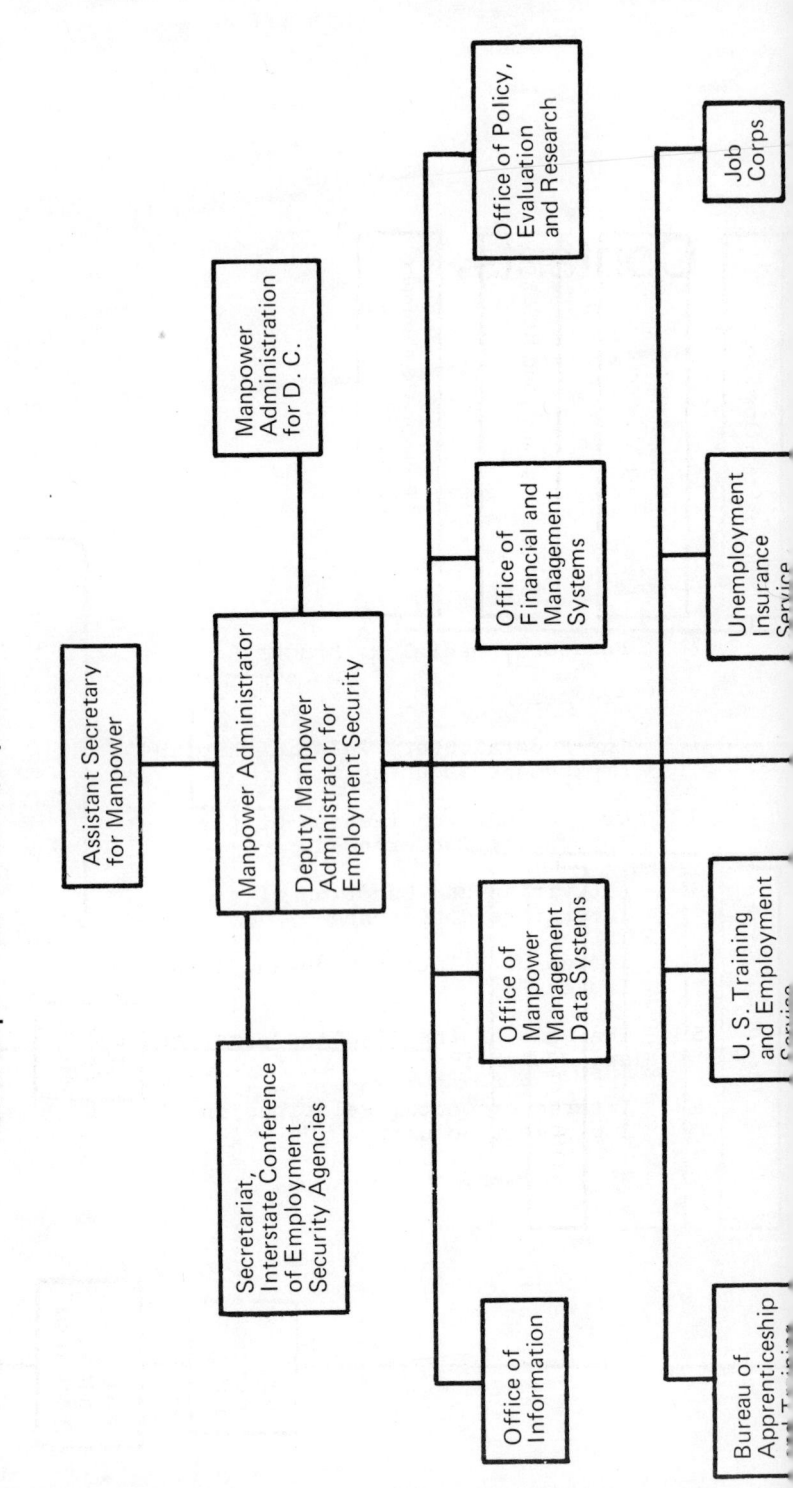

```
                    ┌──────────────────────┐
                    │ Assistant Secretary  │
                    │ for Manpower         │
                    └──────────┬───────────┘
                               │
┌─────────────────┐ ┌──────────┴───────────┐ ┌──────────────────┐
│ Secretariat,    │ │ Manpower Administrator│ │ Manpower         │
│ Interstate      ├─┤                      ├─┤ Administration   │
│ Conference of   │ │ Deputy Manpower      │ │ for D. C.        │
│ Employment      │ │ Administrator for    │ └──────────────────┘
│ Security        │ │ Employment Security  │
│ Agencies        │ │                      │
└─────────────────┘ └──────────┬───────────┘
                               │
   ┌──────────┬────────────────┼────────────────┬──────────────┐
   │          │                │                │              │
┌──────┐ ┌─────────┐     ┌──────────┐     ┌──────────┐   ┌──────────┐
│Office│ │Office of│     │Office of │     │Office of │   │   ...    │
│ of   │ │Manpower │     │Financial │     │Policy,   │
│Infor-│ │Manage-  │     │and Mgmt. │     │Evaluation│
│mation│ │ment Data│     │Systems   │     │and       │
│      │ │Systems  │     │          │     │Research  │
└──────┘ └─────────┘     └──────────┘     └──────────┘

   ┌──────────────┬────────────────┬──────────────┐
┌──────────┐ ┌──────────┐   ┌──────────┐   ┌──────────┐
│Bureau of │ │U. S.     │   │Unemploy- │   │Job       │
│Apprentice│ │Training  │   │ment      │   │Corps     │
│ship      │ │and       │   │Insurance │   │          │
│          │ │Employment│   │Service   │   │          │
└──────────┘ └──────────┘   └──────────┘   └──────────┘
```

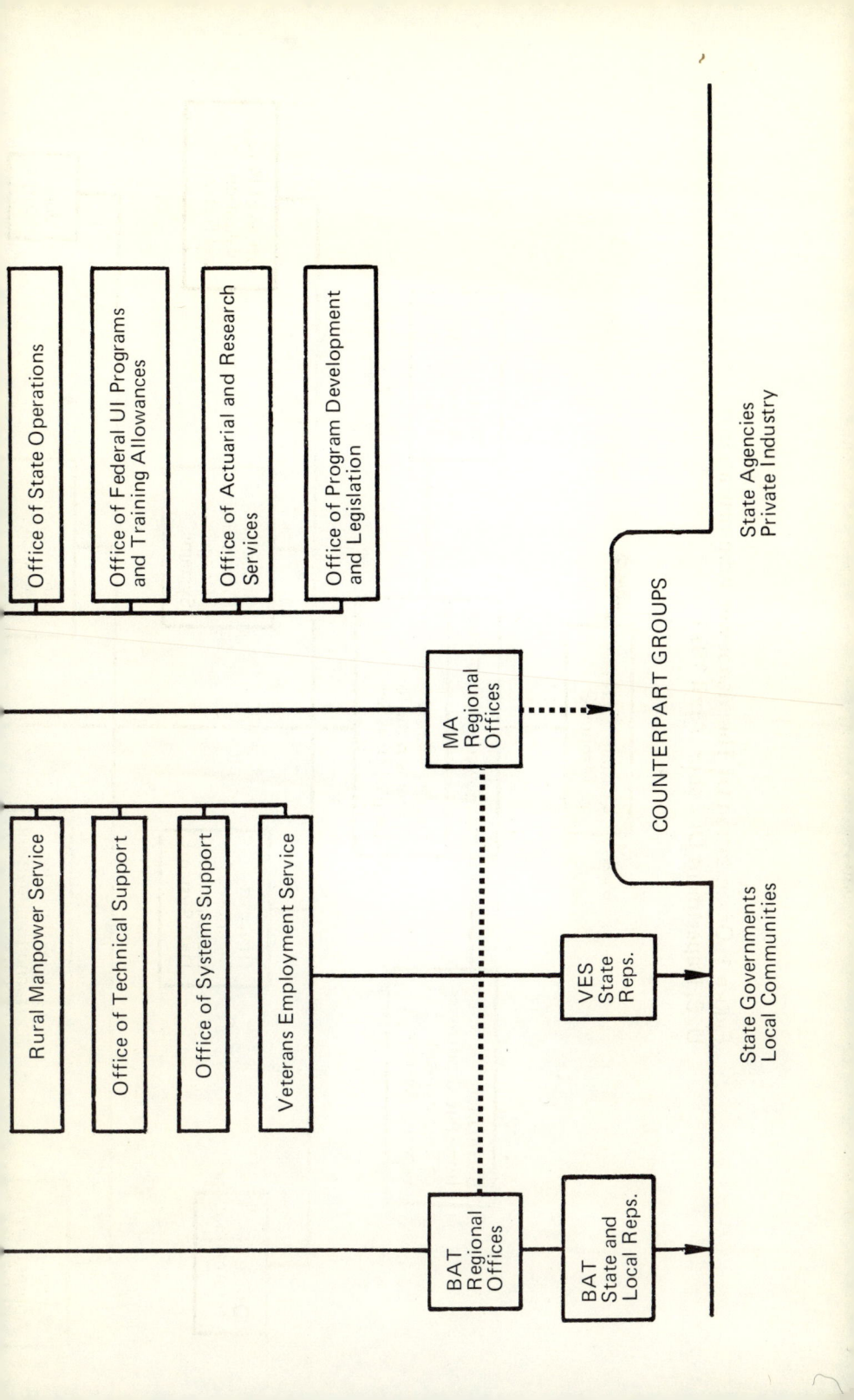

| Office of State Operations | Office of Federal UI Programs and Training Allowances | Office of Actuarial and Research Services | Office of Program Development and Legislation |

| Rural Manpower Service | Office of Technical Support | Office of Systems Support | Veterans Employment Service |

MA Regional Offices

VES State Reps.

BAT Regional Offices

BAT State and Local Reps.

COUNTERPART GROUPS

State Agencies
Private Industry

State Governments
Local Communities

Foreword

This volume deals with an organization, the Interstate Conference of Employment Security Agencies, which played a major role in shaping the federal-state employment security system. The objectives of this system were twofold. One was to facilitate the employment process for those members of the nation's labor force who needed some kind of assistance in their search for employment, for example, counseling, testing, training, and labor market and job market information and referral, functions that are provided through the state employment services. The second objective was to administer and operate the federal-state unemployment insurance system, which pays weekly benefits to eligible unemployed workers.

The Interstate Conference, established in 1937, was an organization of the state employment security agencies. Following the passage of the Social Security Act of 1935, which created the federal-state unemployment insurance program, some of the state unemployment insurance administrators felt the need for an organization to deal with matters of mutual interest and provide a forum for the exchange of ideas and discussions of administrative and policy problems. Between 1935-37 state administrators held discussions as to the kind of organization needed. In 1937, the organization of state administrators came into being under the name of the Interstate Conference of Unemployment Compensation Administration. In 1939 when the U.S. Employment Service was transferred to the Bureau of Unemployment Compensation in the Federal Security Agency, its name was changed to the Interstate Conference of Employment Security Agencies. Although conceived in harmony and cooperation, the activities of the Conference were not always consistent with the position of the Bureau of Employment Security, U.S. Department of Labor, as they related to federal legislation. Usually the battle was over matters that fell under the broad heading of "states' rights."

The funding of the employment security program gave rise to some of the tensions. This federal-state program was financed 100 percent by federal grants, which placed the state administrators in a unique position. Governors generally did not pay much attention to this program because no state funds were involved. However, when the governors did take a position on some aspect of the program, the state administrators could say that federal regulations did not permit the action sought by the governors. Conversely, when the Bureau sought a particular policy or a change in specific legislation, especially as it related to federal standards for unemployment insurance, the administrators raised the states' rights banner. In addition, the Interstate Conference members would frequently lobby with their congressional representatives against the administration's legislative proposals. When this Bureau was dissolved and the Employment Service and the Unemployment Insurance Service became units of the Manpower Administration, tensions appeared to increase.

The Interstate Conference activities were entirely financed by the U.S. Department of Labor. Moreover, the executive secretary and the small staff of the Interstate Conference were full-time employees of the U.S. Department of Labor. This arrangement continued from the early days of the Conference until June 30, 1973.

The Williams study portrays the history of the Interstate Conference from its inception to 1970. This volume is a history and analysis of a unique organization in intergovernmental relationships and Professor Williams has performed a useful contribution. His study focuses on the interaction of the U.S. Department of Labor and the Interstate Conference, its organizational structure, and the technical activities of the committees established by the Conference. Little attention is given, however, to policy implications of the lobbying activities of the Interstate Conference.

These lobbying activities have changed the course of history of the Interstate Conference of Employment Security Agencies. In May 1972, four public interest organizations -- National

Association of Community Development, Council for Community Action, National Association of Social Workers, and National Conference on Public Service Employment -- filed suit in the U.S. District Court in the District of Columbia against the Interstate Conference to halt the use of congressionally appropriated funds for lobbying purposes (Civil Action 1059-72). Defendants in the suit were the U.S. Department of Labor and the Interstate Conference of Employment Security Agencies.

The cause of the action cited by the plaintiffs is 18 USC, Section 1913, which reads:

> No part of the money appropriated by any enactment of Congress shall, in the absence of express authorization by Congress, be used directly or indirectly to pay for any personal service, advertisement, telegram, telephone, letter, printed or written matter, or other device, intended or designed to influence in any manner a Member of Congress, to favor or oppose, by vote or otherwise, any legislation or appropriation by Congress, whether before or after the introduction of any bill or resolution proposing such legislation or appropriation; but this shall not prevent officers or employees of the United States or of its departments or agencies from communicating to Members of Congress on the request of any Member or to Congress, through the proper official channels, requests for legislation or appropriations which they deem necessary for the efficient conduct of the public business.

The civil suit alleged that the defendants violated 18 USC, Section 1913 by utilizing congressionally appropriated funds for extensive lobbying efforts.

The parties in the suit agreed to a dismissal of the case on May 29, 1973. Under the terms and conditions of the stipulation of dismissal the parties agreed and stipulated that effective July 1, 1973:

    (a)   The U.S. Department of Labor will not assign employees to provide staff services for the Interstate Conference of Employment Security Agencies.

    (b)   The U.S. Department of Labor will not furnish office space, other facilities, or directly provide funds for the operation of the Interstate Conference.

    (c)   The parties agree that it is the intent of the U.S. Department of Labor that this termination of support of the Interstate Conference will continue hereafter.

Following this dismissal, the Interstate Conference began discussions with the U.S. Department of Labor as to the future of the Conference. The Conference has incorporated itself as a private nonprofit organization under the laws of Virginia. Its membership will be limited to state employment security agencies. The U.S. Department of Labor will increase the administrative grants to the states by $4,000. Such funds are being authorized to be used to support the Interstate Conference. The Manpower Administration authorized the voluntary use of grant funds by state agencies for membership fees in professional organizations and associations. According to the Manpower Administration (General Administration Letter No. 1493, dated July 30, 1973), this authorization included the Interstate Conference of Employment Agencies. Whether all states will participate in the reconstituted Conference remains to be seen. State laws may well restrict expenditures of funds for such purposes.

The states' fees will be used by the Conference to employ a staff, rent office space in Washington, D.C., and provide the necessary funds for its operations. The organization will perform the following functions: consult with and provide technical, programmatic, operational, and other advice to the U.S. Department of Labor in matters concerning employment service, unemployment compensation, and other related manpower matters. Moreover, it will continue to provide reports of its committee meetings to member state agencies.

This dramatic turn of events resulting from the filing of the court case and subsequent dismissal has indeed changed the course of the Interstate Conference of Employment Security Agencies. Professor Williams has traced the history and the activities of the Interstate Conference, which provide the backdrop for current developments. The Interstate Conference has played an important role in the evolution of the federal-state employment security program in the United States. Given the dynamics of this system, if the Interstate Conference had not been established on the initiative of state agency administrators, in all probability it would have been established by law. There is a critical need for an effective mechanism that encourages interaction and interfacing between the administrators of the U.S. Department of Labor and the state employment security agencies. Such an organization is essential to creative federalism.

                      -- Daniel H. Kruger
                          Michigan State University

Preface

The developments in employment and unemployment are critical, and the federal-state employment security and manpower system is an important factor. The Interstate Conference of Employment Security Agencies (ICESA) has been both lauded and lambasted for its influence in the employment security system. This study, however, presents a description and an analysis of the intergovernmental relationship in the employment security system and its administrative and political consequences. Instead of approving or disapproving specific policy positions of the Interstate Conference, the study emphasizes the general political and administrative impact of the Conference. in order to provide both practitioners and students with a better understanding of this intergovernmental relationship.

Since the most visible ICESA activities, which are used the most frequently for evaluation, are also the most controversial, an understanding of the full range of activities and impact may lead to a more accurate assessment. As a detailed case study of cooperative interstate and intergovernmental techniques which partially bridge the federal bifurcation, the study could also be useful to those examining other intergovernmental relationships.

Appreciation and acknowledgement are sincerely extended to the Council on Graduate Education for Public Administration of the American Society for Public Administration and the Civil Service Commission. These organizations provided the Public Administration Fellowship that supported much of the research for this study, including a two-year period spent by the author as a participant-observer with the Executive Secretary of the ICESA and the U.S. Department of Labor, his attendance at two ICESA annual meetings and most standing and special committee meetings, and observation of internal decision-making processes. Appreciation is particularly given to Gerald A. Foster, ICESA Executive Secretary, his staff, and other ICESA officials for their extensive cooperation and valuable assistance; officials of the Manpower Administration and the former Bureau of Employment Security, U.S. Department of Labor; and the typists of many drafts, my wife, Mary, and Carol Sue Cummins.

1
The Federal-State Relationship in Employment Security

An important factor in the success or failure of employment security, manpower, and related programs in the United States is the intergovernmental mechanism through which most of these programs are administered. More specifically, the problems of policy-making and administration in the diverse but interdependent functions of the federal, state, and local units are critical when confronting developments in employment and unemployment. An important participant in this intergovernmental relationship was the Interstate Conference of Employment Security Agencies (ICESA), an organization of state agencies which was structured and operated in a rather unique fashion.

Focusing on intergovernmental relationships in the employment security and manpower system, this study investigates the cooperative bases of the relationship, the sharing of leadership and decision making, and the administrative and political consequences. Important questions that are considered include the following: What was the role of state and national governments in the system? Was power shared? In what ways, to what extent, and by whom? Did the states become mere administrative extensions of the federal government? Did grant-in-aid relationships in the employment security system function only as channels for federal influence over state actions or also as channels through which state influence was felt at the federal level? Was the popularly perceived trend toward federal centralization balanced in part by more covert methods of power sharing? Since federalism is a device for dividing power, what were some of the ways in which the needs for integration and coordination, particularly in areas of common concern and responsibility were met? How were some of the benefits of decentralization retained in the general trend toward centralization? What were some formal and informal adaptations and institutions for furthering cooperation? What was the role of informal cooperative relationships in the operation of the system?

Organization for Manpower Functions

The objectives of the employment security system are to promote employment opportunities through employment assistance and training and to minimize the effects of unemployment through unemployment insurance. The system is organized to meet these objectives at both state and federal levels; an employment service (ES) supplies the jobs and related employment training and assistance, and unemployment insurance (UI) compensates eligible workers for a portion of their wage loss when they are unemployed. Employment service functions include training programs, job placement, testing, counseling, occupational analysis, labor market information, employability development, industrial services, and assistance to special groups such as farm laborers, older workers, veterans, minorities, the disadvantaged, and the handicapped.

The federal counterpart to this system is the Manpower Administration (MA) in the U.S. Department of Labor. Major MA subunits include the U.S. Training and Employment Service (USTES), the Unemployment Insurance Service (UIS), the Bureau of Apprenticeship and Training (BAT), and the Job Corps. Although these and other federal units illustrated in Figure I are concerned with policy development, determination of conformity to federal requirements, allocation of monies, clearinghouse and service functions, prescription of statistical reporting requirements, research, and technical assistance, they are not engaged in actual program operations. Operations are carried out under the direction of the state agencies. Program relationships funnel down to the state employment security agencies in an hourglass pattern of authority. They are fanned out again from these semi-independent agencies and programs are implemented.

For over twenty years, the federal end of the employment security system was the relatively autonomous Bureau of Employment Security (BES). In the early sixties, however, a Manpower Administration was formed as a coordinating superstructure over the various manpower activities in the Department of Labor, including the BES. This overlay created duplicate administrative functions and competition between the traditionally semi-autonomous bureaus. Therefore, repeated reorganizations which generally centralized various bureau functions at the Manpower Administration level were precipitated. The full-scale 1969 reorganization eliminated the bureaus and established their previous functions directly under the Manpower Administration. This reorganization terminated the long-standing relationship between the BES and the state agencies, which is studied here in detail. The reorganization also presents some excellent insight into the responses and operation of the system during the reorganization attempts, at the time of reorganization, and following the reorganization in the transfer of old relationships and the establishment of new ones. The roles and responses of the BES, the state agencies, and the Interstate Conference during this period are most useful in developing an understanding of the operation of the system and the intergovernmental relationship.

The state portion of the federal-state employment security system, now in operation more than thirty years, is the state employment security agencies, which include all fifty states, The District of Columbia, Puerto Rico, The Virgin Islands, and Guam. In most respects, each state designs its unemployment insurance program. The amount and duration of benefits, eligibility requirements, coverage, and tax rates are generally decided by state legislative action. The federal portion of the system provides advice and assistance, acts as a clearinghouse, recommends federal UI legislation, and determines, within Congressional appropriations, the amounts needed by the states to administer the state laws. The federal role in unemployment insurance has always been a controversial subject and federalization of the system and federal UI standards are very touchy issues.

While the states make many of the substantive decisions on standards and benefits in unemployment insurance, there is a tendency for employment service activities and programs to be federally initiated and controlled. A large part of employment service activities is carried out by the states under the federal Wagner-Peyser Act, but many special programs which are closely directed from the federal level have been added. These programs include the Manpower Development and Training Act (MDTA), the Area Redevelopment Act (ARA), the Concentrated Employment Program (CEP), various Economic Opportunity Act programs, and supportive services to programs such as The Job Corps and The Neighborhood Youth Corps. The redirection of employment service efforts toward the disadvantaged and those with special employment problems, for example, has been induced largely by the federal level.

Historical Conditioning of the Intergovernmental Relationship

The design of the employment security program was largely a result of the Depression and developments in legal, political, and social thought. After discussing many possible systems, the Committee on Economic Security, created in 1934 by President Franklin D. Roosevelt, recommended a compromise national-state employment security system. The committee suggested that the role of the national government should be confined to promoting state action, managing the reserve fund, and assisting the states; the primary responsibility for legislation and administration would belong to the states.[1] Edwin E. Witte, chairman of the committee, commented that the creation of the system was largely influenced by the inability of the members to agree on the provisions of a federal law and the feeling of many that the Supreme Court and Congress would not support a national system.[2]

A portion of the system was already operative through enactment of the 1933 Wagner-Peyser Act, which offered federal matching funds to states having employment offices. In 1935 Title III of the Social Security Act added a system of unemployment compensation to be administered through the public employment offices and provided a common financial basis for both unemployment insurance and the employment service.

The Social Security Act provided for a federal payroll tax of three percent on covered employers with the provision that employers who paid a tax to a state with an approved law could use the state tax as an offset, up to ninety percent against the federal tax. All states, thus induced, set up the appropriate systems. The act also provided that state administrative costs would be financed by a 100 percent grant from the national percentage. The taxes paid to the state are earmarked for each state and put in the Unemployment Trust Fund in the federal treasury.

During its thirty years of operation, there have been some important organizational changes in the employment security program at the federal level and in the relationship with the state agencies. The federal units of the system have been transferred and reorganized several times so that the relationship has not been continuous with one federal unit. When the system was created, the Bureau of Unemployment Compensation was under the Social Security Board and the United States Employment Service was in the Department of Labor.[3] Reorganization Plan No. 1 in 1939, prepared by the President and approved by Congress, created the Federal Security Agency and placed the Social Security Board within that agency. The plan also transferred the USES and consolidated it with the Bureau of Unemployment Compensation in the new Bureau of Employment Security under the Social Security Board.[4]

During World War II, the state employment services were federalized under the War Manpower Commission. At the request of the President and with the understanding that federal administration would continue only for the duration of the war, the governors in 1942 transferred the administration of the public employment offices to the federal government in order to expedite national industrial mobilization. After the war, however, the federal government appeared reluctant to return the employment services to the states. This became a controversial issue, and in the governors' conferences of 1944, 1945, and 1946, the governors urged their return. The public employment offices were finally returned to the states by an act of Congress in November 1946.

In 1945 when the War Manpower Commission was abolished through an Executive Order by President Harry S. Truman, the employment service at the federal level was placed in the Department of Labor instead of being returned to the Social Security Board, thus separating it again from unemployment insurance. Congress, however, rejected the President's 1948 reorganization plan which would have made the transfer under the Executive Order permanent. When Congress included a provision in the Federal Security Agency appropriation transferring the U.S. Employment Service back to the Social Security Administration, the President vetoed the bill, but it was passed over his veto. In 1949, Reorganization Plan No. 2 transferred both the employment service and unemployment insurance activities from the Social Security Administration to the Department of Labor.[5]

Since the transfer in 1949, the employment service and unemployment insurance have remained in the Department of Labor. These functions were under the Bureau of Employment Security until 1969 when the BES was eliminated and they were placed directly under the Manpower Administration.

The Fiscal Context

The grant system is an important factor in the federal-state employment security relationship. The costs of administration are borne by appropriations from one level of government (federal) and the actual administration is carried on by the other level (the states). The traditional and main source of funds is the Federal Unemployment Tax Act (FUTA) payroll tax on employers, which is collected and put in the Unemployment Trust Fund held by the U.S. Treasury. Appropriations are made from this fund by Congress for both federal and state administration of the program. Since the tax is earmarked, any excess not appropriated is retained in a loan and reserve fund arrangement. Monies granted to the state agencies for unemployment insurance and employment service administration (not including employment insurance benefits or other allowances distributed through the system) have increased markedly in recent years; grants to states have increased from $400,000,000 in 1963 to $806,000,000 in fiscal 1972.

A greater influence than the growth of grants to states for ES and UI functions, however, has been the significant and dramatic increase in other new programs and sources of funds. From $56,070,000 in 1963, new programs and their funding have increased to a total of $1,360,183,000 in 1970 for programs including the Manpower Development and Training Act (MDTA), Neighborhood Youth Corps (NYC), Operation Mainstream, Public Service Careers, Special Impact, Concentrated Employment Program (CEP), Job Opportunities in the Business Sector (JOBS), Work Incentive Program (WIN), and Job Corps. The employment security system, once the main manpower program of the federal government, has seen other competing organizations and programs established.
The transformation from being <u>the program</u> to becoming <u>a part</u> of the manpower program was traumatic in many ways for the employment security program in the federal Department of Labor, in the state employment

security agencies, and in related organizations
such as the Interstate Conference of Employment
Security Agencies. As discussed later, the growth
and change in manpower programs is critical to
some of the problems and relationships in the
system.

Fiscal arrangements are a major basis of
federal control in the system. It is important to
reiterate that the employment security program is
for all practical purposes entirely financed by
funds under federal control. As an early student
of the system observed, federal control of funds
tends to make the state an agent and the federal
government the principal.[6]

In the process of allocating funds for state
administration of the program (not including benefits), each state submits a detailed budget request
for administrative funds including appropriate
justifications, organizational charts, descriptions
of functions and activities, and staffing patterns.
Budgets are closely reviewed by the federal regional staff, and, after a second review at the national
level, funds are apportioned to each state. Details
such as the number of positions allotted to a
specific activity are authorized and controlled at
the federal level; there is no general grant of
funds to the state. As might be expected, such
close fiscal control creates problems in the intergovernmental relationship and necessitates a closer
administrative relationship between the jurisdictional sections.

System Inducements and Controls

Any relationship between organizational units is dependent in many ways on the response and control repertoire of each unit. The ultimate fiscal sanction is rarely applied, but the federal government may withdraw administrative grants and deny credit against the federal unemployment tax if a state is found to be in noncompliance with the federal law. A survey by the ICESA Legislative Committee indicates the rare use of this device: seventeen states reported a total of twenty-six conformity issues over the history of the program, but in only two cases were grants withheld.[7] A lesser sanction that requires the restoration of funds is the audit exception for improper expenditures.

Fiscal control is also an important key to other management and program controls. For example, detailed federal approval of state staffing by position and job specifications is controlled in large part through budget allocations. The same, of course, is also true of policy control and development. Although the states have a large amount of control with respect to unemployment insurance, policy direction in employment service activities is very heavily influenced by the federal partner. A projected fiscal 1969 deficit, for example, was used by the national government to modify policy and redirect employment service resources through review, approval, and adjustment of state plans of service and budget requests. Such actions are often handled through consultation, but the fiscal arrangement permits the federal government to "consult" from the strong position.

The federal control of employment security operations is substantial. The broad base of this fiscal and administrative control is the federal authority to ensure "proper and efficient administration" under Title III of the Social Security Act and to withhold funds for noncompliance under the Wagner-Peyser regulations issued by the Secretary of Labor. Other federal roles important to control are those of technical assistant, consultant, interpreter, evaluator, and auditor.

Federalism in Employment Security

The extent of federal control warrants the statement that the employment security federal-state relationship is not a voluntary-advisory relationship between two government units but rather a hierarchical one tempered by structured decentralization to the state. Although many assessments of the system have been favorable,[8] the influence of federalization and the extent of the federal role have been important issues throughout the history of the system, and they continue to be a source of tension and suspicion. As one long-time observer has noted: "Federal-State relations have probably been more tense for a longer time in Employment Security than in any other department of government."[9] The Kestenbaum Commission on intergovernmental relations stated that the role of the national government had been unduly extended through administrative controls (although it felt the federal role had been too restricted in unemployment insurance benefit standards and some other substantive areas).[10] The management consultants to the commission recommended certain changes in the employment security federal-state relationship, including the discontinuation of the detailed budgeting system and control over organization, staffing, procedures, and equipment.

Although the employment security system was conceptually a system of partners, in operation the states appeared in many ways to be administrative agents of the federal government and to this extent subordinate to it. The states were separate and important units in the system with areas of latitude such as unemployment insurance benefits. However, administrative and fiscal mechanisms provided the federal level with substantial control in many areas. In addition to the formal distribution of functions, the state agencies were able to gain access to decision centers and increase their influence through a variety of arrangements. The Interstate Conference of Employment Security Agencies and other mechanisms were important means through which the state agencies gained control and influence. These matters are the subjects of later chapters.

The Employment Security System as a Case in Intergovernmental Relations

How can the intergovernmental relationship in the employment security system be described most accurately? Is it a case of cooperation or conflict, coalition or competition? Is it similar or significantly different from other intergovernmental relationships? Has it changed over time? Survey research provides insight and indicates important questions for further investigation.[11] In order to compare employment security perceptions at different times and with other groups engaged in intergovernmental relations, a 1968 questionnaire answered by federal and state employment security officials duplicated some questions from survey studies on intergovernmental relations by Edward Weidner, the Muskie Subcommittee on Intergovernmental Relations, and Francis Rourke.[12] Although rigorous comparisons are severely limited, the comparative responses roughly indicate some interesting points for further discussion.[13]

Comparative Cooperation

State officials in general perceived national officials to be very cooperative.[14] State employment security officials also indicated a high degree of cooperation with respect to the Bureau of Employment Security. It is significant that most respondents in each survey felt the cooperativeness of the national level to be either very good or good; seventy-nine percent of all state officials and ninety-two percent of state employment security officials gave such a rating. It is interesting that state employment security officials see the national government as somewhat more cooperative than do other state officials.

Balance of Power

The Muskie Subcommittee survey and the employment security survey included duplicate questions dealing with the perceived power balances in intergovernmental relations.[15] One question inquired whether the United States was becoming "too centralized." Slightly more state employment security officials than state officials in general responded that power in the United States was becoming too centralized. With respect to whether the present system of federal grants caused an unbalanced emphasis in state and local programs, there was no difference in employment security and other state responses.

TABLE 1

Selected Comparisons Between the Muskie Subcommittee and Employment Security Surveys*

Subject and Responding Officials	Yes	No
Too Centralized		
General state (Muskie)	60.0%	40.0%
State employment security (1968)	69.3	30.7
State Imbalance Created by Grants-in-Aid		
General state (Muskie)	63.9	36.1
State employment security (1968)	63.1	36.9

*Only those responding to this question in each study are compared; all totals equal 100.0%.

Mitigation of Controversy

Three questions taken from the 1952 Rourke study allow some comparison of officials in the employment security program over time.[16] The responses roughly indicate the following: First, federal officials, at least in these instances, are not representative of the perceptions and opinions of state employment security officials.[17] Second, there seem to have been changes over time. Third, the change between 1952 and 1968 (in the questions used for comparison) seems to be toward mitigation of controversy.

More specifically, almost three-fourths of

those responding in 1952 indicated that difficulties in intergovernmental relations were inherent in an administrative system such as the employment security system, where fiscal responsibility was vested in the national government while policy control rested largely with the states. In the 1968 study slightly over one-half of the federal officials -- but seventy percent of the state officials -- indicated that this was so.

The 1968 responses to another question also suggest a significant decrease in controversy since 1952. Three-fourths of the respondents in the Rourke study indicated that the controversy over federalization of the program had hindered the development of better relations between the national and state agencies because it had made the states unduly suspicious of national proposals for improving the program; in 1968 around one-half held this opinion.

In reply to the statement that the main activity of the ICESA "has been political activity and it has done comparatively little to improve the administration of the program," there was also a decided change in responses over time. The 1952 responses were quite evenly divided, while only 20 percent of the comparable BES officials in 1968 agreed. These responses indicate that there had been marked changes in the perceptions of the ICESA and its role in the employment security system.

TABLE 2

Selected Comparisons Between the 1952 Rourke and 1968 Employment Security Surveys*

		Yes	No	Undecided
Inherent Difficulties in Intergovernmental Relations				
1952 survey		73%	21%	6%
1968 survey	Federal	55	32	13
	State	70	13	12
Controversy over Federalization as a Hinderance to Better Relations				
1952 survey		76	15	9
1968 survey	Federal	58	26	13
	State	63	27	9
ICESA Activity Political Rather than Improving Administration				
1952 survey		42	46	9
1968 survey	Federal	21	68	11
	State	11	76	12

*Since the 1952 survey covered only federal officials, the direct comparison is with the 1968 survey of federal officials. All totals equal 100 percent when those not responding to this question are added.

Sources of Tension

The attitudes of employment security officials also appear to differ from those of the general state officials surveyed by Edward Weidner.[18] With respect to national government activities in the respondent's area of responsibility, slightly more national employment security representatives than officials at large replied that activities should be expanded. In another question significantly more state officials in the Weidner study than in the employment security study felt that the attitude of national administrative officials toward their agency was primarily one of assistance. On the other hand, significantly more state employment security officials described it as an attitude of inspection and direction. Even though many differences may account for the variation, the comparison indicates that the relationship in the employment security program is perceived as less one of assistance than one of inspection and direction. In an intergovernmental situation, more conflict and a less satisfactory relationship might thus be expected.

When asked whether national technical advice and assistance should be increased or decreased, it is significant that there seems to be less satisfaction with the present situation in the employment security system. Almost all respondents were dissatisfied with national technical assistance, half wanting an increase and half a decrease. The majority in the Weidner study wanted no change.

The Weidner respondents and state employment security officials emphatically agree that supervision by national administrators should not be increased, although more in the Weidner survey were satisfied with no change. To the question of whether state officials had less "say-so" as a result of contacts with national administrators, most Weidner responents indicated that it made little difference. Most state employment security officials said they had less say-so, but many said it made little difference. Significantly more state employment security officials felt their relative power and control diminished by federal contacts. In a final comparison, different responses are given to the question whether funds would be allocated differently if federal grants had no strings attached. Sixty percent in the Weidner study answered that they would not allocate differently. Significantly, eighty-nine percent of the state employment security officials replied they would allocate funds differently than presently allocated by the federal government. This series of responses seems incongruent with the high cooperative rating given earlier and indicates some disagreements that might result in conflict rather than in cooperation.

TABLE 3

Selected Comparisons Between the Weidner and Employment Security Surveys

Questions	State Officials in General	State Employment Security Officials
Expansion of National Activities		
Yes	59%	64%
No	37	36
Attitude of National Officials		
Assistance	56	37
Inspection	14	26
Direction	13	36
National Technical Advice and Assistance		
Increase	27	50
No change	59	8
Decrease	9	41
National Supervision		
Increase	6	1
No change	65	49
Decrease	25	47
Less State Control Resulting from National Contacts		
Less	29	54
No difference	61	43

Cooperation and Conflict

The comparative responses in this section suggest both a higher rating of cooperativeness and a wider basis for dissatisfaction and conflict in the employment security system. A central question is: How are the sources of tension, dissatisfaction, and conflict handled in the system to the extent that the participants perceive the system to be cooperative?

CHAPTER I
FOOTNOTES

[1] U.S. Commission on Intergovernmental Relations, <u>A Report to the President for Transmittal to the Congress</u> (Washington, D.C.: U.S. Government Printing Office, 1955) p. 198. See also William Haber and Merrill G. Murray, <u>Unemployment Insurance in the American Economy; An Historical Review and Analysis</u> (Homewood, Illinois: Richard Irwin, 1966) pp. 398 ff.

[2] Edwin E. Witte, <u>Social Security Perspectives</u>, ed. Robert J. Lampman (Madison: University of Wisconsin Press, 1962) pp. 286-87.

[3] In its October 1938 meeting, the Interstate Conference of Unemployment Compensation Agencies, later to become the ICESA, favored unification of the two units under the Social Security Board.

[4] See Arthur J. Altmeyer, <u>The Formative Years of Social Security</u> (Madison: University of Wisconsin Press, 1966) p. 117.

[5] <u>Ibid</u>. pp. 154, 163-64, 176-79. Apparently the ICESA did not take a position either for or against this transfer.

[6] Raymond C. Atkinson, The Federal Role in Unemployment Compensation Administration (Washington, D.C.: Committee on Public Administration, Social Science Research Council, 1941) p. 4.

[7] Haber and Murray, Unemployment Insurance in the American Economy, pp. 446-47. The question of compliance came up again recently in a California proposal to reorganize the employment service in that state; testimony of Department of Labor officials in California legislative hearings indicated that the proposed organizational structure would probably not be in conformity, thus resulting in the withholding of funds. The extremity of such possible action induced changes acceptable to both parties.

[8] Witte, Social Security Perspectives, p. 242; U.S. Congress, House Select Subcommittee on Labor of the Committee on Education and Labor, The Role and Mission of the Federal-State Employment Service in the American Economy, 88th Congress, 2nd Session (1964) pp. 49-57; ICESA, Annual Meeting (1955) p. 3; and see, for example, ICESA, Annual Meeting (1953) p. 9; (1962) p. 19; (1950) p. 31.

[9] Joseph Becker in Interstate Conference of Employment Security Agencies, Annual Meeting (1955) p. 20.

[10] Commission on Intergovernmental Relations, Report, pp. 198-211, especially pp. 200-201.

[11] At the federal level, questionnaires were sent to the top Bureau of Employment Security national office officials, including the heads of the Bureau, service and office levels, and to all BES regional administrators. At the state level, questionnaires were mailed to all state administrators and to the heads of the employment service and unemployment insurance offices in each state. In addition, questionnaires were sent to all the state persons serving on an Interstate Conference committee and to the Bureau and regional consultants to each committee not included above. Of the 297 total questionnaires, 211 were returned (71%) and 197 were completed and returned in time for the computer tabulations. Since this type of data is limited, the data are used more for verification, illustration, and insight than for statistical significance in the narrow sense of the term. In addition, the survey was taken in 1968 prior to the reorganization of the Manpower Administration. For a copy of the questionnaire, more complete data and tables, methodological discussion, composition of the sample, and tests of representativeness, see David G. Williams, Cooperative Intergovernmental Relationships: The Interstate Conference of Employment Security Agencies (Ph.D. dissertation, Graduate School of Public Affairs, State University of New York at Albany, 1970) pp. 20-26, 228-33 (available from University Microfilms, Ann Arbor, Michigan, #70-25,487, in film or Xerox copy).

[12]Edward W. Weidner, Intergovernmental Relations as Seen by Public Officials (Minneapoli University of Minnesota Press, 1960); U.S. Congress, Senate Subcommittee on Intergovernmental Relations of the Committee on Government Operations, The Federal System as Seen by State and Local Officials, Results of a Questionnaire Dealing with Intergovernmental Relations, 88th Congress, 1st Session (1963); and Rourke, Intergovernmental Relations in Employment Security. See also the 1955 survey reported in U.S. Congress House Committee on Government Operations, Replies from State and Local Governments to Questionnaires on Intergovernmental Relations, 85th Congress, 1st Session (1957).

[13]Comparability is limited by sample selection and size, difference of time and reference, and variance in program and structural factors.

[14]Weidner, Intergovernmental Relations as Seen by Public Officials, pp. 50-51.

[15]Senate Subcommittee on Intergovernmental Relations, The Federal System as Seen by State and Local Officials, pp. v, xi, 35 ff., 183 ff.

[16]Rourke, Intergovernmental Relations in Employment Security, pp. 107, 110-13, 118.

[17] Some have maintained that the extensive experience of federal employment security officials at the state level has made them more understanding and representative of that level. Of the federal officials surveyed, 61 percent have worked at the state level. There appears to be little movement in the reverse direction.

[18] Weidner, *Intergovernmental Relations as Seen by Public Officials*, pp. 29, 92-95. With respect to national expansion in all functional areas, only 18 percent felt that national activities should be expanded, and 75 percent felt they should not.

2
Origin and Organization of the Interstate Conference

A rather unique organization, the ICESA supplemented the official intergovernmental relationship in employment security. The ICESA cannot be easily classified; it had a broader scope of activities and power than a professional organization and its membership was markedly different.[1] A recent evaluation of the employment service called the ICESA "the trade association, lobbyist, spokesman and negotiator for the employment service network."[2] It was similar to an interstate compact or agreement in some aspects, but in other ways it functioned as a private interest group. As will be discussed later, the ICESA performed some functions necessary for an adequate national employment security system, which could not be accomplished by the federal partner without additional authority. The ICESA was similar to national organizations of state officials in other functional fields, but somewhat more extensive in operation. It was an organizational affiliation with a unique financial base.

Origin and Development

After the passage of the Social Security Act in 1935 and the enactment of state unemployment compensation laws in the following two years, some officials felt a need for a voluntary state organization to deal with matters of mutual interest, improve federal-state and interstate coordination, and provide an exchange of ideas and a discussion of administrative and policy problems.[3] There was an important need for a device to accomplish administratively some activities that otherwise could not be either easily or legally accomplished. Arthur Altmeyer, then chairman of the Social Security Board, writes that since the system was federal-state rather than wholly federal, some additional organization or arrangement was necessary to perform some functions.[4]

Of the seven states that had enacted unemployment compensation laws by the end of 1935, four (New Hampshire, Massachusetts, Connecticut, and New York) met in New York City on December 28, 1935 to discuss problems that had already arisen and to plan reciprocal agreements between the states. The chairman of the Social Security Board and two other board officials also attended the meeting. Since it was agreed that another meeting should be arranged, the chairman of the Social Security Board was requested to call a meeting of state unemployment compensation officials in the Eastern Atlantic States. The subsequent meeting was held in Washington, D.C. on January 23, 1936. After a discussion of technical problems, the five states present decided to maintain informal contacts to exchange information and develop some uniformity in administrative detail. The Bureau of Unemployment Compensation of the Social Security Board endorsed this purpose and offered to assist.

Nine states were represented at a third meeting, held in New York City on February 21-22, 1936. The director of unemployment insurance for the state of New York, who presided at the meeting, explained that the conference was called to further consider a voluntary and cooperative state effort "toward the further unification of standards, procedures, interpretations, and even amendments to the various laws." The creation of a formal organization was again considered at a fourth meeting, held in Washington, D.C. on May 21-22, 1936 and attended by representatives from ten states. Officials of the Social Security Board assured the state agencies that it would cooperate in and assist such an effort.

At a subsequent meeting in New Hampshire on July 23-25, 1936, six committee reports were presented and the organization began to take more definite shape. A resolution was adopted creating a Committee on Organization to consider alternative arrangements for a continuous interstate relationship. A further step towards full organization was taken by the fourteen states present at a meeting in Madison, Wisconsin, on October 21-23, 1936, when five standing committees were created, and procedures on voting, the calling of meetings, and other matters were developed.

At a March 17-19, 1937 meeting, thirty-nine states and the District of Columbia (and various federal officials) heard the report from the Committee on Organization and its proposal for an Interstate Conference of Unemployment Compensation Administrators. The proposal was accepted, Mr. Morris Dunne of Oregon was elected president, and a committee was selected to draft a constitution. At the request of the president (in a precedent-setting action), a member of the federal Bureau staff was designated as executive assistant to the president of the Conference. The executive secretariat continued to be staffed and financed by the federal government.

The first meeting of the new organization was held in October 1937, under the name Interstate Conference of Unemployment Compensation Agencies. In October 1939, when the United States Employment Service was transferred to the Bureau of Unemployment Compensation in the Federal Security Agency, the title was broadened to the Interstate Conference of Employment Security Agencies.[5]

Article II of the Interstate Conference Constitution stated that the objectives of the Conference were the effectiveness of unemployment compensation laws and employment service and manpower training programs, promotion of employment security, fostering of close professional relationships, proposal of new federal and state legislation through study and research, exchange of ideas among administrators, encouragement of research, and promotion of proper and efficient methods of administration.[6] The initial cooperation and harmony in the achievement of these objectives, however, soon foundered as the Bureau and Conference viewpoints diverged on various topics, and Conference activities expanded. A state administrator and president of the ICESA noted:

> The Conference was conceived primarily as a professional-technical organization, concerned with the administrative problems of launching a new program under an untried Federal-State cooperative arrangement. Soon thereafter, jurisdictional problems began to arise and, through necessity, the Conference began to gradually assume a more important and vital role as it related to both internal operations and legislation bearing upon various aspects of the program.[7]

Another former president of the Conference characterized the relationship more colorfully:

> The Interstate Conference is to my mind a unique and relatively young organization, a child of a shotgun wedding, the offspring of parents as jealous as notorious. Its home life, other than its earliest years, has not been either very happy or congenial. Nevertheless, its life has been filled with much controversy and action which has made of it a very proud and independent child--loved by some, despised by others, unknown to most. The paternal parent, although never to the best of my knowledge having disclaimed it entirely, has wished many times that it could.[8]

The child once born and blessed proved to be both a boon and a burden to the federal parent. The ICESA was often an important support and communications channel, but it took opposing positions on administrative and legislative matters. Expansion of the areas of concern and increased controversy in the relationship can also be noted from the ICESA annual meetings. The early meetings were almost totally concerned with program development and detailed administrative problems, while those in more recent decades generally concentrated on overall program, political, and legislative matters.

Organization and Affiliation

The ICESA was an independent organization comprised of member state employment security agencies. Other than the close relationship to the federal level, it was not affiliated with other organizations. Discussions of associating with the Council of State Governments were closely connected to the desire for an organizational and financial base independent of the federal government. These possibilities were investigated as organizational changes in the Department of Labor Manpower Administration posed problems and uncertainties. For example, the ICESA Committee on Conference Organization in 1967-68 investigated association with the Council and also organization as an interstate compact; no action beyond initial contacts was taken.

As suggested by its title, the ICESA was an organizational rather than a personal affiliation. There was no certification of or provision for

personal membership, although delegates from each
member agency were designated to the annual meeting.
Participation in ICESA activities was not limited
within the state employment security agency, but
was generally confined to the top officials at
the state level. In practice the state administrator nominated for committees and otherwise loosely
approved and controlled the participation of his
subordinates. The only restriction on ICESA office
holders was employment by one of the member state
agencies for at least one year.

As an official organization, the ICESA functioned through its annual meeting, which was held
in September or October of each year. Three
delegates from each state were authorized to attend
the annual meeting in addition to the Conference
officers. Other interested persons such as federal
officials and representatives of management and
labor also attended. In recent years, a mid-year
meeting of state administrators was also held.

Conference Officers

The elected officers of the Conference were the
president, senior vice-president, past president
(by virtue of his previous election), and regional
vice-presidents. The president was often a state
administrator. The office of senior vice-president,
initiated in 1968, was intended to train the incoming president, although elevation to that office
was not automatic. The office of past president
was intended to give some continuity to the officers, and an unsuccessful attempt was made to
delete the office when a senior vice-president was
added in 1968. The treasurer, an office with

virtually no meaningful duties, was deleted in the major revision of the constitution in 1970.

There were a number of ICESA regional changes in past years. For the 1968-69 Conference year there were thirteen ICESA regions (not the same as the federal regions) each with a regional vice-president; beginning in the 1969-70 conference year there were only six regions, but two vice-presidents with overlapping terms from each region. An extensive revision of the ICESA constitution in 1970 created ten ICESA regions concurrent with the federal Manpower Administration regions, with one vice-president from each region. This ICESA regional change enabled more meaningful activity at the regional level at a time when the Department of Labor -- for other reasons -- was decentralizing much authority and responsibility to that level. Although the ICESA constitution provided for regional executive committees headed by the regional vice-president, they generally were not operative. These complementary actions by the ICESA and the Department of Labor facilitated more ICESA contacts and impact at the regional level. The National Executive Committee, composed of the president, senior vice-president, past president, and the regional vice-presidents, was the continuous operating and directing body of the Interstate Conference. It had "all powers necessary to effectuate the objectives" of the Conference.[9]

Executive Secretary

One of the most important officers was the executive secretary, a unique and interesting position that was important to both the ICESA and the federal government, particularly the old Bureau of Employment Security. At the request of the first ICESA president, a staff member of the federal Bureau was assigned to serve as his executive assistant and to act as liaison between the Conference and the Bureau.[10] The executive secretary continued as both an official of the state agencies' organization and a career federal employee. The Conference constitution and code provided that the executive secretary was to be financed through the Bureau of Employment Security and was also to be attached to the administrator of that Bureau. For many years in the BES, the executive secretary was also the Special Assistant for Federal-State Relations attached directly to the administrator. The reorganized Manpower Administration, which made the ICESA executive secretary an assistant to the manpower administrator, has forced some important informal changes.

The executive secretary did not play as important or extensive a role in the Manpower Administration as he did in the BES. When the executive secretary functioned as a principal assistant to the Bureau administrator, the dual nature of the position gave him powerful influence and informative ability for both the state and federal governments. After the Manpower Administration reorganization, however, the executive secretary was not generally relied upon as a top staff assistant dealing with the state agencies; rather, he was generally limited to ICESA functions. Although he was consulted on program matters and included pro forma in some staff meetings, his role in policy and as a principal aide was greatly decreased.

It is an important and rather unique factor that the federal government provided funds, office space, and personnel for the executive secretariat of an independent state organization. As will be more fully discussed later, expenditures for ICESA activities are allowed from funds granted to the state employment security agencies. Thus, ICESA activities and operations were also indirectly financed by the federal government.

Being an agent both for a state organization and for a federal agency created some problems, but it generally provided the executive secretary with a powerful focal position. One long-time state administrator and past ICESA president attributed many of the accomplishments of the Conference to the status of the executive secretary, indicating that his dual role did not hinder his effectiveness or reliability.[11] The arrangement fostered close coordination and access for both the states and federal employment security agencies to the top policy and administrative processes of the other.

Recent legal action has been directed toward the use of federal funds for what is considered lobbying activity. This has indirectly stimulated actions that will probaby result in the federal government granting funds to the state agencies to support the executive secretary and staff rather than continue direct federal support. This would result in some major changes in relationships and operations of the executive secretary.

The National Executive Committee designated the executive secretary each year, but this was usually only a formal continuation of the current secretary. The initial selection included both ICESA and BES participation. Although the ICESA constitution provided that the authority, duties, and responsibilities of the executive secretary and the manner of his appointment shall be designated in a written agreement between the federal government and the ICESA, no such agreement existed. The operation and appointment of the executive secretary was essentially a matter of state-federal cooperation. Changes in funding will probably make the executive secretary solely a state employee.

In many ways, the staff or executive secretariat of an organization is a powerful and guiding influence. There is no clear-cut line between policy and administration, or staff and line. Therefore, the choice of ICESA executive secretary was important for the operation of the Interstate Conference. In many respects, as Department of Labor organizational changes were made, many of the old informal relationships with the Executive Secretariat did not carry over into the new formal organizational arrangements.

Conference Committees

A major portion of the work of the Interstate Conference was accomplished through its standing and special committees that covered most areas of substantive concern in the employment security program. In the 1970-71 Conference year, for example, there were sixteen regular committees staffed by 139 people. In addition, special committees were often formed during the year with additional state representation. Most committees met one to three times a year, although some met as often as six or seven times when needed. Detailed reports of the meetings were distributed to the states and served as an important informative device for the state agencies.

In addition to the participation of federal personnel in the committee meetings as requested, most committees had both a national and regional consultant; twelve national and nine regional office consultants were assigned to eleven of the sixteen committees in 1970-71. For example, the head of the Unemployment Insurance Service and the head of the United States Training and Employment Service were consultants to committees in these areas. This arrangement is indicative of the close and generally constructive working relationship between the committees and the federal level, including its administrative and technical staff.

The range of ICESA Committee activities and their areas of substantive concern is illustrated by the regular 1970-71 Conference committees:

  Administrative Financing Committee
  Automated Manpower Systems Committee
  Benefit Financing Committee
  Employment Service and Manpower Committee
  Family Assistance Program Committee
  Information and Education Committee
  Interstate Benefit Payments Committee
  Legal Affairs Committee
  Legislative Committee
  Minority Group Relations Committee
  Research and Reporting Committee
  Rural Manpower Committee
  Training Committee
  Unemployment Insurance Committee
  Urban Affairs Committee
  Veterans Committee

Throughout the years of the Conference's existence,

there was an impressive amount of committee work. Appendix A lists the ICESA committees from 1937-71; Table 4 summarizes the number of ICESA committees and their general areas of concern. Over time, the emphasis of committee attention seems to have been on unemployment insurance from the standpoint of the number of committees. This is not unexpected since the early concern of the Conference was unemployment insurance, and the committee structure traditionally divided the unemployment insurance area into several specific committee assignments while the employment service area was served by fewer and more general committees.

In addition to the regular committees, special committees were created as needed during the Conference year. In 1967-68, for example, an Ad Hoc Committee on the 1969 appropriation was established to consult with the Bureau on how a budget deficit should be handled, a Planning Committee on Employment Security Financing met with Chairman Wilbur Mills of the House Ways and Means Committee to discuss funding problems, and another ad hoc committee reviewed MDTA reporting requirements.

Financing the Interstate Conference

Since the state employment security agencies are financed by federal grants, there are no separate funds outside federal control to adequately support an organization of state agencies. ICESA activities were financed from grant allocations as a normal part of the state agencies' activities; there was no separate allocation to the state agencies for ICESA activities. Most ICESA expen-

TABLE 4

General Areas of Concern of ICESA Committees
1937-71

General Program Area	Committee-Years
Unemployment Insurance	**125**
Unemployment insurance	36
Interstate benefit payments	37
Financing of benefits	26
Benefit coverage	21
Fraud	5
Employment Service	**59**
Employment service	38
Farm labor	21
Administrative, Staff and Fiscal	**118**
Grants and financing	50
Reports and records	31
Management improvements	16
Personnel	21
Miscellaneous	**141**
General employment security concerns	9
Legislative	31
Community matters	8
Veterans	27
Minority groups	3
Legal matters	23
Conference organization and operation	9
Public relations	14
Other	17
Total	443

ditures were covered by one of the state agencies on a cooperative basis, and no funds were pooled by the states for ICESA purposes. For example, most Conference supplies such as letterheads and envelopes were printed at the expense of one of the state agencies (generally the one administered by the current ICESA president). This financial arrangement required close federal-state cooperation since most expenditures and travel had to be approved simultaneously by the state agency, the ICESA, and at the federal level.

Due largely to the extensive committee activities, the most sizable Conference expense was travel and per diem costs. In recent years, travel and per diem expenses were authorized both by the Manpower Administration and ICESA, either in a general schedule of meetings at the first of the year or subsequently during the year as needed. Travel and per diem costs in 1967 were $115,729.21; the average yearly cost of a recent ten-year period (1958-67) was $94,001.02. Even though this amount is large, it should be noted that many of the meetings and activities, which might otherwise have been sponsored by the federal level, were sponsored by the Interstate Conference. To this extent, the difference may be one of accounting rather than financing since the funds flowed from the same source and were used for many of the same purposes. Incidental expenses other than travel and per diem, such as the duplication and distribution of the ICESA committee reports, were not reported separately and were absorbed by the various state agencies and the federal level.

The largest single expense was the ICESA annual meeting; travel and per diem costs accounted for $45,770.00 of the $115,729.21 total travel and per diem expense for 1967. The costs of the meeting itself were covered by the registration fee and the host state agency. If the state had little budget flexibility, the federal government sometimes allowed a small supplementary grant to that state for the purpose of hosting the meeting.

The financial basis of the Interstate Conference has been severely criticized, especially by those generally in opposition to Conference political activities and legislative positions. Two long-time students of the system, William Haber and Merrill Murray, wrote:

> It is rather paradoxical that the Interstate Conference, representing the legislative and political interests of the states, is financed by a Bureau of a federal department with whose legislative objectives it is frequently in conflict.[12]

In effect, some complained, this arrangement was a financial subsidy enabling state agencies to lobby and take actions that were often contrary to the aims of the granter.

This argument was the basis of a recent lawsuit against the ICESA by the National Association for Community Development, the Council for Community Action, the National Association of Social Workers, and the National Conference on Public Service Employment. Although the suit has not yet been resolved, it probably has been the stimulus to make a major change in the funding process. The federal Office of Management and Budget has taken initial actions to discontinue direct financing of the ICESA executive secretary and his office. Instead, $200,000 has been included in the budget request for grants to the states to fund the secretariat. This is a major change in relationships and funding; the ICESA will probably have to find private quarters and the staff would no longer be federal employees.

Organized labor was especially critical of the ICESA financial arrangement; its representatives questioned the arrangement within the Department of Labor, the Federal Advisory Council, and before the U.S. Congress.[13] Most of the criticism was directed toward ICESA federal legislative activities, and both congressional committees and the Federal Advisory Council expressed concern in this respect.[14]

There were few conflicts between the Department of Labor and the ICESA on travel and per diem expenses for the meetings of the standing committees and special committees; there were a few instances of disagreement over the ICESA annual meeting, however. The Secretary of Labor did not approve the site or conditions of the meeting in a few cases. For example, Secretary Wirtz objected to the 1967 meeting scheduled for Hawaii since the money demands of the Vietnam war were high and it would have been more expensive to meet in Hawaii than in the continental states.[15] Secretary Mitchell objected to holding the annual meeting in Las Vegas. In 1941, because of the war expense, the Social Security Board wanted only one delegate per state to attend the annual meeting. The Executive Committee wanted three delegates but

43

was willing to let the Social Security Board designate the classes of officials to attend. The Board decided to allow three delegates -- the state administrator and the heads of ES and UI -- but said it would only approve one delegate per state in the future. Accordingly, the 1942 meeting had but one delegate per state.[16] The issue -- one of the nullification of ICESA Constitutional procedures by the federal partner -- was generally not pressed by the Conference, probably because the financial arrangements were largely controlled by the federal government. In this form, the issue arose only a few times and was generally resolved by ICESA acquiesence, often with protest or negotiation.

As with the federal government, this semi-dependent financial relationship was not always satisfactory to the ICESA. Although the arrangement generally worked well, there were attempts from the first to find an independent source of financing. In the 1940 annual meeting, the ICESA president reported little success on the mandate of the Conference to the Executive Committee to find methods of independent financing.[17] An attempt in 1968 included contacts exploring affiliation with the Council of State Governments and contacts with congressmen about the possibility of forming an interstate compact. Arrangements were not necessarily static and were the result of incremental changes; further changes are likely to be made as a result of the recent lawsuit. The financing of the executive secretariat which began rather informally will be discontinued. It appears, however, that federal funds granted to the states will be used for ICESA staff and activities.

Unique Intergovernmental Agent

As illustrated in this chapter, the Interstate Conference of Employment Security Agencies was a somewhat unique agent in the employment security intergovernmental relationship. As a state organization financed by federal funds, in many ways it was a supplement to the regular line relationship of the federal Manpower Administration and the state employment security agencies. Although it was an extra-hierarchical arrangement, its activities and relationships included the top federal and state employment security personnel. Extensive committee activities under its sponsorship covered almost all aspects of the employment security relationship and provided federal-state discussion of employment security and manpower programs and policies. Building on the above discussion of Interstate Conference development, organization, and financial basis, the following chapter will discuss its operations and functions.

CHAPTER II
FOOTNOTES

[1]The professional association in this area is the International Association of Personnel in Employment Security (IAPES).

[2]*Falling Down on the Job: The United States Employment Service and the Disadvantaged* (n.p.: Lawyers' Committee for Civil Rights Under Law and the National Urban Coalition, June, 1971) p.88.

[3]The minutes of the early annual meetings serve as the general source for the following discussion of the origin of the ICESA; in particular see ICESA, *Annual Meeting* (1943) pp. 91-92.

[4]Arthur J. Altmeyer, *The Formative Years of Social Security* (Madison: University of Wisconsin Press, 1966) pp. 21-26.

[5]See Fred C. Croxton, "The Interstate Conference of Employment Security Agencies," *Employment Security Review*, Vol. 7 (December, 1940), pp. 14-16; Francis E. Rourke, *Intergovernmental Relations in Employment Security* (Minneapolis: University of Minnesota Press, 1952), p. 76; and, William Haber and Merrill G. Murray, *Unemployment Insurance in the American Economy: An Historical Review and Analysis* (Homewood, Illinois: Richard Irwin, 1966) p. 456.

[6] Interstate Conference of Employment Security Agencies, Constitution and Code (As Amended Through September 25, 1970), Art. 2. See also "Interstate Conference of Employment Security Agencies," Encyclopedia of Associations, Vol. I: National Organizations of the United States (Detroit: Gale Research Co., 1964) p. 323.

[7] Fred Garrett of Idaho, ICESA, Annual Meeting (1953) pp. 13-14.

[8] Bernard Teets of Colorado, ICESA, Annual Meeting (1952) p. 101.

[9] ICESA, Constitution and Code (1970), Art. VII, Sec. 1.

[10] See U.S. Department of Labor, Federal Advisory Council on Employment Security, Committee on Bureau Relations with the Interstate Conference, Report (October 3-4, 1956). See also ICESA, Annual Meeting (1943) pp. 42-93. Miss Kathryn Fenn was selected as the first Executive Secretary. She was replaced in 1942 by R. Brice Waters; Joseph W. Hathcock succeeded Mr. Waters in the midst of the 1944-45 Conference year and served until the 1947-48 Conference year when Dr. William R. Curtis was selected. Gerald A. Foster succeeded Dr. Curtis during the 1958-59 Conference year.

[11] Samuel Bernstein of Illinois, ICESA, Annual Meeting (1957) p. 10.

[12] Haber and Murray, Unemployment Insurance, p. 459.

[13] "A Job on the Jobless," I.U.D. Digest (Industrial Union Department, AFL-CIO), Vol. 3 (Summer, 1958) pp. 10-19, especially p. 12. See also John Herling, "Aborting Federalism," Washington Daily News, July 26, 1966, p. 23.

[14] See the appropriation requests and Congressional committee comments in House Report No. 228, Senate Report No. 265, and Conference Report No. 892 of the 1st Session of the 81st Congress; House Report No. 228 and Senate Report No. 410 in the 84th Congress, 1st Session; and House Report No. 1845, 84th Congress, 2nd Session. See also the discussion on this subject with the BES Administrator in U.S. House Subcommittee of the Committee on Appropriations, Departments of Labor and Health, Education, and Welfare Appropriations for 1967, 89th Congress, 2nd Session (1966), 89th Congress, 2nd Session (1966) pp. 389-90.

[15] ICESA, Annual Meeting (1966) pp. 8, 11-12, 48-59.

[16] See ICESA, Annual Meeting (1941) p. 9.

[17] ICESA, *Annual Meeting* (1940) p. 100.

[18] ICESA, *Annual Meeting* (1959) pp. 42-43.

3
Activities and Function of the Interstate Conference

Most participants at the top levels in the employment security system feel that the participation and influence of the ICESA greatly increased the influence of the state agencies in the federal-state system, where the federal government has long been the stronger partner. In the 1968 survey of top federal and state employment security personnel, over three-fourths indicated that state influence in the system was increased. In a related question on the degree of ICESA impact, over ninety percent rated the ICESA influence at various degrees of significance; only five percent rated it as insignificant. In his 1952 study of the employment security intergovernmental relationship, Rourke concluded that "there seemed to be general agreement among these officials that the achievements of the Interstate Conference had been substantial."[1]

Direct Channel for Consultation

In a certain sense the ICESA did not exist as an organization in and for itself, but as a technique for arranging regular contacts between the jurisdictional halves of the employment security system. The ICESA mechanism, unlike the hierarchical relationship through the federal regions, allowed for direct national-state contacts and consultation without the encumbrances of the regular channels. The executive secretary, whose organizational location has provided participative access into the top echelons of both organizations, was a significant aid to this direct consultation. However, although still included in the formal policy clearance process, the role of the Executive Secretary in the informal policy process was not as extensive in the Manpower Administration as under the Bureau of Employment Security.

Collective Voice

A significant aspect of the ICESA is that it facilitated the combining of the state agencies into collective action and voice. Although there was naturally some dissension within the Conference, the state position in discussions and negotiations was significantly strengthened overall by this collective action. At the same time, the Conference was careful not to deny any state its individual voice. The ICESA constitution provided that "no member agency shall ever be deprived of its rights or privileges to assert its own position on any issue."[2] Official Conference positions on major issues could be taken only after a poll of the state agencies; the National Executive Committee and other committees, however, could operate and take positions in their respective areas of competence. Since the committees were deliberately constructed with geographical and population considerations, their deliberations generally represented a collective state position.

The collective voice of the state agencies proved to be especially influential with respect to federal legislation. Writing on the unemployment insurance program, Haber and Murray noted:

> The Interstate Conference has undoubtedly exerted a powerful influence on the unemployment insurance program. As the collective voice for the state administrators, its views have great weight with Congress. Since its leadership has usually been conservative, it has often successfully opposed Administration proposals for liberalization of the program. It has also frequently served as a collective bargaining agency for the state agencies when issues have arisen between the Bureau for Employment Security and the state agencies.[3]

The power of this collective voice is also negatively recognized by a labor columnist in the Washington Daily News:

> Organized 30 years ago--when the Unemployment Insurance law was enacted--to create a bridge of understanding and cooperation between the Federal and state governments, the association has degenerated into a booby trap, which has tripped up the Truman, Eisenhower, Kennedy and now the Johnson Administrations.[4]

The ICESA also served as a combined state agency voice in relationships with other groups such as veterans organizations, the President's Committee on Employment of the Handicapped (whose Executive Committee includes one ICESA designee), and the Federal Advisory Council to the Department of Labor on the employment security program (whose related meetings could be attended by the ICESA president).[5]

Cooperative Mechanism

One of the significant aspects of the ICESA was its regularization and institutionalization of cooperation and consultation. As stated at one of the early ICESA annual meetings, it "justifies its existence only inasmuch as it fosters and encourages this indispensable cooperation."[6] In this regard, two questions were relevant for both the state and federal levels: What is the extent of participation? How "cooperative" is the relationship? In the 1968 survey, almost all of the top state and federal officials indicated extensive participation in ICESA activities; less than three percent had not participated. As a group, state agency administrators were especially active in ICESA matters. Other top state officials were active in ICESA matters but slightly less so. Regional and national BES officials generally indicated moderate activity.

Given that participation in ICESA activities was quite extensive, how did the federal and state agencies perceive this participation? How cooperative did they feel their counterparts to be?

Almost all federal and state officials felt that
the other level cooperated well with them; almost
ninety-two percent rated it good and very good,
only seven percent rated it fair or poor, and none
rated it very poor. It is interesting to note in
the comparison of subgroups that national officials
perceived state officials to be more cooperative
than did the state officials in their perception
of national officials. Regional officials, who
worked directly with the state agencies, ranked
the states especially high in cooperativeness,
and state administrators were somewhat more positive in their ranking of national cooperativeness
than the ranking by other state officials.

Influence on the Policy Process

Through the ICESA, the state agencies were able
to increase their participation in the formulation
of administrative and program policy. A memorandum
from the administrator of the Bureau of Employment
Security indicated the extent of this participation:

> Virtually all significant legislation,
> programs, policies, rules and regula-
> tions, and frequently implementing
> instructions have been discussed
> with regular or special committees of
> the Conference on which senior members
> of the Bureau staff are consultants
> in an attempt to make them as acceptable
> as possible . . . the Conference machinery
> can generally be relied upon to produce
> a reasonable consensus and to assist in
> implementation. It has worked well and
> we would propose no change in this
> method of consultation except to
> strengthen it where possible.[7]

Much of this cooperative consideration of policies,
programs, and operations took place in the substantive committees, the National Executive Committee,

and special committees as created. The substantive committees were given specific assignments from the National Executive Committee, but could investigate, discuss, and recommend with respect to any area within their competence. Since national and regional consultants as well as other appropriate federal personnel participated, committee meetings were the place where policies were discussed and sometimes finalized.

Prior to the reorganization, policy consultation was generally limited to the Bureau of Employment Security and the Manpower Administration officials. On occasion, however, it also included other parts of the Department of Labor. When the Work Incentive Program (WIN) of the 1967 Social Security Amendments (administered through the state employment security agencies) was assigned to the Bureau of Work Training Programs (BWTP), an ICESA committee was formed and met with representatives from BWTP, BES, and HEW. In the series of meetings, the WIN program implementation and design were discussed, and significant changes were made. Largely on the basis of committee arguments and suggestions, the financial system was extensively modified, the comprehensive plan of operation was changed from sixty-two detailed pages to a more flexible seven pages, reporting instructions and forms were standardized and made compatible with existing requirements, and the contractual agreement was markedly changed to reflect state organizational arrangements.

That committee recommendations met some success is also illustrated by the Employment

Service and Manpower Committee's review of the disposition of the recommendations made in a previous year. Of the twenty-one major recommendations made in 1967, fifteen were accepted and implemented, four were no longer applicable, and two had been rejected.

The Conference has not only discussed and advised, but has on occasion also initiated consideration and adoption of policies. A reinsurance plan for unemployment insurance in the event of catastrophies was developed by the ICESA Benefit Financing Committee.[8] Committee reports and recommendations are often noted by authorities in the field with respect to many programs and issues.[9]

Part of the decreased involvement of the executive secretary in the policy process resulted from the increased direct contacts of the Assistant Secretary of Labor and Manpower administrator with the state agencies rather than using the ICESA as the contact point. Another important cause was the expanded and reorganized Manpower Administration and the limited scope of the Interstate Conference; that is, manpower resources, programs, and agencies increased so that the Manpower Administration functions covered programs and agencies broader than the Interstate Conference. At first, the ICESA and the BES were involved in a one-to-one program and organizational relationship and the ICESA had a greater impact; but eventually the ICESA was but one part of the administrative constituency and program of the Manpower Administration.

These relationships were not static, but there appeared to be less give and take than in the relationship with the Bureau of Employment

Security. In the unemployment insurance area the
Conference was extensively involved in legislative
and policy development, including work on the
unemployment trigger provision and implementation
of wage combining provisions. It was in the manpower area, however, where much of the change lay.
Although the Manpower Administration had carefully
explained legislation, the Conference did not par-
ticipate to any great extent in the development of
legislation. Reacting to this, the Interstate
Conference was active in preparing its own proposals for manpower legislation.

Process for Technical Review and Comment

Supplementing the broader policy issues, the ICESA
provided a process to review and comment on more
specific and technical issues. In addition to
the recommendations stemming from committee
meetings, there were more formal technical review
and comment processes. The most formalized review
process was the clearance by the Manpower Administration with the ICESA Research and Reporting
Committee of reporting and statistical requirements prior to their issuance. Reports that concerned another committee, such as unemployment
insurance, were also cleared with the chairman of
the committee. Although the Conference in the
final analysis could not negate a federal proposal,
opposition raises serious questions and generally
induces further discussion and negotiation. This

clearance procedure generally allowed the operating portion of the program -- the state agencies -- to review reporting requirements, keep such requirements minimized, improve reports with respect to the operating level, include state needs and viewpoints, and raise operational questions. The clearance procedure also served to help ensure the funding of reporting requirements; in fact, an agreement was reached with the BES that each new reporting requirement must state the necessary funds available for its accomplishment in order to be issued. This clearance process, though small in the general perspective, has been important to the research, reporting, and program areas. In 1966 the ICESA Research and Reporting Committee reviewed over thirty-five separate reports; the 1968 committee reviewed ten new or revised reports in addition to two special meetings devoted to the reporting requirements for the MDTA and WIN programs respectively.

Another important arrangement that fostered ICESA influence in the policy review process was the clearance of federal policies and official issuances by the ICESA executive secretary in his federal capacity. As an assistant to the Manpower Administrator, the executive secretary was involved in the formal clearance of federal policy issuances. In his dual capacity, he could consult with the states and bring policy matters to their attention both formally and informally before their issuance and could include state reactions in his clearances and modifications.

Cooperative Management Device

An especially effective method for cooperative management of selected undertakings that was used in recent years is the joint ICESA-federal steering committee and task force. Joint steering committees with authority to direct development and implementation and to make policy decisions were set up in several management improvement areas where federal-state cooperation was particularly necessary for effective results. One committee and its task forces directed the development and implementation of an employment security automatic data processing system, including giving detailed guidance to the contractor assisting in the development of the system. Both the steering committee and the task forces were co-chaired by ICESA and federal representatives.

Still another committee, predecessor to the automatic data processing committee, was established to update the general management of the grants system, including management information, plans of service, cost management, and evaluation systems. A good illustration of the cooperative accomplishments of the committee is the self-evaluation system in which the state agencies evaluated their own accomplishments against a plan of service; federal monitoring helped to ensure objective evaluation processes. Monitoring of a state process is a significant departure from the federal evaluation that might have been expected without cooperative formulation of the system, and the management capacity at the state level was improved rather than making it less responsible.

A part of the concept of the joint steering committee was the extensive use of selected model states in testing new approaches and developing parts of the various programs for the entire system. The developments in the model states were under the direction and evaluation of the joint steering committees. After the model state systems were developed and tested, they were modified as needed and exported to other states.

Through these cooperative steering devices, the states added their voices and perspectives to the developments in various areas of common concern. The ICESA, therefore, served as a collective mechanism to work with the federal partner in the development and implementation of solutions to common needs; individual states would be unable to develop such compatible and national systems, and a federally designed system would not include the necessary information from the operational level and would have to be imposed on the states. The ICESA was a natural mechanism to facilitate this cooperation.

Interstate Arrangements

The ICESA also served as a vehicle to accomplish many activities that could not otherwise be adequately handled either by individual states or by the federal government. In some important areas, neither the states nor the federal government had legal authority for action. For example, interstate cooperation in benefit payments, appeals, fraud activities, reciprocal coverage, audits, and collections were all handled on a cooperative interstate basis. Although these arrangements were similar in many ways to an interstate compact and the 1968 ICESA Committee on Conference Organization investigated that possibility, they were not established by congressional action and were inferior to state legislative action.

The most extensive interstate arrangement was the ICESA Committee on Interstate Benefit Payments and the various interstate agreements on the uniform treatment of claims and coverage for workers operating across state lines.[10] The Committee had the authority to implement the various interstate benefit plans; prescribe uniform interstate benefit procedures, forms, and regulations for all participating states; aid in adjusting differences between states; and evaluate the operation of the interstate benefit payments program. Since the Interstate Benefit Payments Committee was a committee of state people with no separate secretariat, the federal level furnished some technical assistance and served as a coordinating and distributing point.

The interstate agreements under which the Interstate Benefit Payments Committee had responsibilities included the Interstate Benefit Payment Plan, Interstate Plan for Combining Wages, Interstate Reciprocal Coverage Agreement, and the Consolidated Wage Combining Plan. By action of the National Executive Committee, the Committee also had the responsibility for the Interstate Maritime Reciprocal Agreement. These interstate plans covered unemployment insurance matters that could not be handled under individual state systems such as the payment of benefits to unemployed individuals absent from the state in which benefit credits have accumulated, coverage when an individual worked in more than one state for one employer, combining wage credits when the individual had worked in more than one state, continuity of coverage to maritime workers, and other contingencies. Each plan, of course, required individual state agreement and not all states participated in all plans. The Consolidated Interstate Plan for Combining Wages was developed in recent years by the Interstate Benefit Payments Committee to further reduce inequities in interstate claim matters. This plan was endorsed by the 1968 annual meeting and a resolution was passed urging individual state adoption.

Medium of Interstate Communication

The ICESA was also an important channel for communication among the states themselves; it provided a large portion of the formal and informal occasions for the representatives of the different states to meet and exchange ideas. The ICESA channel of communication was particularly important as an independent and supplementary alternative that was separate from the regular hierarchical channels. The publication and distribution of the committee minutes, for example, provided an important independent state (rather than federal) channel of information on current developments in each program area.

One committee almost solely concerned with communicating useful information to the state agencies was the Legal Affairs Committee, formerly the Attorneys Exchange Committee, which provided an exchange of legal views, indexes and digests of significant decisions, and legal opinions.

Legislative Activities

Perhaps the most controversial ICESA activities were those with respect to national legislative proposals. Since this was often the most visible ICESA activity to those outside the employment security program, many saw the ICESA primarily as a lobbying organization. Critics complained that such activities were not proper because the federal grant would thus subsidize political activity and lobbying that was often contrary to national proposals. Much of the evaluation of ICESA legislative activity seems to depend on whether or not the evaluator and the Conference agreed on issues. The Conference was both blamed as an obstructive employer's influence, and blessed as the protector of states' rights and the employment security system.[11]

Federal legislative issues are usually controversial among the states themselves, and the ICESA Constitution provided that "neither the President or any other official of the Conference, acting in an official capacity, shall make any attempt to prompt the administrators of the State agencies or other groups to attempt to influence members of Congress."[12] Whatever this provision of the Constitution meant -- it is probably a response to criticisms and the legal restrictions against lobbying -- it did not seem to prohibit extensive ICESA activity with respect to members of Congress and national legislative proposals. Conference positions on federal legislative issues could be expressed to Congress after they were determined by vote in the annual meeting or by an interim poll of the state agencies. Until recent years, the positions of the individual state agencies on legislative matters were known only to the executive secretary -- a federal employee -- who tabulated the poll. Obviously this put the executive secretary in a difficult position. A number of years ago during ICESA testimony in a congressional hearing regarding state positions on legislation, the executive secretary was called to testify and give information about the positions of the individual states. He said that although he was a career federal official subject to Congress, he could not disclose in good conscience the individual state positions, only the total vote, since these were ICESA provisions. He responded that his orders from the federal government did not contravene the orders from the ICESA, and that he served the ICESA at the pleasure and direction of the federal government. The constitution was subsequently amended to provide that individual state agency positions on legislative (though not nonlegislative) matters may be made known to interested parties.[13]

Examples of ICESA legislative activity are numerous. The Conference testified yearly before both the House and Senate appropriation committees, although as an outside witness rather than as a government witness. In the past, the ICESA was generally an important support for the Bureau of Employment Security in defending their common budget request and was instrumental in restoring budget reductions both through testimony and private contacts with individual congressmen.

Good illustrations of ICESA legislative importance and voice are the hearings of the Ways and Means Committee in 1966, which had the sole purpose "to receive further recommendations on H.R. 8282, Employment Security Amendments of 1965, from Representatives of the Interstate Conference of Employment Security Agencies."[14] This 150 page document is composed of the testimony of nine ICESA representatives and letters from other administrators. The ICESA position was hotly debated by the federal Department of Labor.

The ICESA also has been active in proposing legislation to Congress. For example, a bill prepared and sponsored by the ICESA was introduced by Congressman Wilbur Mills in the 88th Congress. The bill would have provided for the payment of extended benefits during recessions on an automatically triggered basis. Detailed amendments to the Manpower Development and Training Act were suggested in 1967. The ICESA was largely responsible for the introduction and passage of H.R. 272 (extension of the Reed Act) in the 90th Congress. This bill was unopposed, but not of high priority to any except the state employment security agencies; without the constant shepherding and promoting of the bill by the Conference, it probably would not have been reported out of committee. The Conference was active and effective in the initiation, development, and passage of the Employment Security Amendments of 1970. After its passage the Conference and the Unemployment Insurance Service cooperated in preparation for implementation of the amendments. An ad hoc committee of the ICESA studied further modifications in the amendments, particularly modifications in the trigger provisions.

With respect to manpower legislative attempts, the Interstate Conference has not been involved to any great degree in the development of federal legislative proposals, although they have been presented and explained to the Conference. Differing in some respects with the legislation introduced by the administration and with congressional modifications, the Interstate Conference went to extensive lengths to prepare alternative proposals. An ICESA ad hoc committee prepared a statement of principles for manpower programs, the principles were cleared by the state administrators in their mid-year meeting, and a work group of the legislative committee drafted a bill that was presented to the full legislative committee and then to the National Executive Committee for approval and modification. With the passage of the Public Service Employment Act of 1971, the bill was revised.

In its legislative activity, the ICESA was quite effective. While questioning two state employment security administrators, Senator Joseph Clark of the Senate Subcommittee on Employment, Manpower, and Poverty (Committee on Labor and Public Welfare) commented that the ICESA was a very effective lobby, which is listened to carefully. Off-the-record comments of the senator then illustrated how the Conference had had an important effect on a recent employment service bill. This effectiveness is probably due largely to relationships that most state administrators have with their congressional delegations and their respective governors. Since many state administrators are political appointees, they naturally have good political contacts. ICESA officials and members were very active testifying at congressional hearings and contacting individual congressmen in promoting ICESA legislative objectives.[15]

Due to disagreement over the proper role of the ICESA in federal legislation, the federal-state relationship was often strained and difficult. The Conference was criticized because of its "hold" on the Bureau of Employment Security; anticipating opposition, the Department of Labor has had bills introduced without prior consultation with the ICESA.

Organized labor was an important critic of ICESA legislative activity. Labor has tended to be more liberal while the ICESA has been more conservative on the federal role and changes in unemployment insurance and employment service activities. Labor officials criticized the ICESA for being dominated by employer interests.[16] A long article in the IUD Digest (AFL-CIO Industrial Union Department) dealt very critically with the ICESA and its activities and relationships with lobbyists and other private groups. The article was particularly critical of the ICESA's close link to the Unemployment Benefit Advisors (UBA), an employer-supported interest group.[17] The effectiveness of the UBA, the article continued, might have been largely attributed to its "use" of the ICESA in promoting employer objectives. The article further disparaged the ICESA for illegal lobbying through its use of federal money for per diem and travel expenses in lobbying activities.

It is generally true that the Unemployment Benefit Advisers had close contacts with the Interstate Conference; it is also generally true that, when positions of the many organizations involved in legislative battles were drawn, the UBA and the ICESA were often in allied and cooperating camps. These general ideological agreements were helped by the fact that the head of the UBA was generally recruited from past state administrators who had been ICESA presidents. Contacts and continued relationships are to be expected under these circumstances. In addition, the UBA often sponsored events for and met with the state administrators when they were in Washington, D.C. on ICESA or other matters. The UBA offices are in the same hotel where many state agency administrators traditionally stay. These types of contacts and reciprocal support arrangements are influential, but not unusual for government agencies and private organizations.

The propriety of ICESA legislative activities also attracted the concern of the Federal Advisory Council on Employment Security. In 1954, labor members of the Federal Advisory Council charged the ICESA with using federal grants for travel to Washington to lobby against federal legislation proposed by the Bureau. After much discussion, the Advisory Council adopted a report recommending a Bureau policy governing federal legislative activity by state administrators and restricting them to the proposal of legislation and the presentation of views to their own state's congressional delegation, other congressmen at their request, and public hearings.

The BES adopted these recommendations with some minor changes, but a member of the Federal Advisory Council, who was active in preparation of the report, indicated that this did not restrain ICESA congressional activities to any noticeable degree.[18]

Although ICESA congressional activity was somewhat controversial in the circles close to the employment security system, it generally was not a widespread public issue. Only a few articles in general publications appeared on this issue. John Herling of the Washington Daily News wrote that the slow rate of improvement in the unemployment insurance system is due to "obstructionist tactics of a little known group called the Interstate Conference of Employment Security Agencies."[19] He continued that in spite of the willingness of many state administrators to accept federal revisions in unemployment benefits, a "low-level consensus" is manipulated by a few conservative administrators in the ICESA to stop any such modifications.

While the ICESA took positions by votes of the states, it is probably an accurate genralization that the more powerful, numerous, and active state administrators in the ICESA to stop any such modifications.

The most important recent challenge was the lawsuit to prohibit the use of federal funds for ICESA activities which the plaintiffs felt were lobbying activities and thus illegal. The suit has probably led to a change in the funding and organizational relationships although it has not been resolved in the courts. This change may satisfy the plaintiffs, but it probably will not prohibit these activities since the funds may be considered to take on state rather than federal character after they have been granted. The major change will be that a federal official will not be engaged in assisting these activities.

While the ICESA took positions by votes of the states, it is probably an accurate generalization that the more powerful, numerous, and active state administrators in the ICESA tended to be those who leaned toward the more conservative side. In particular, there were a number of state administrators who were in the program for many years and tended to be quite powerful and effective in Conference affairs and leadership. In recent years, however, there was a marked decline in the percentage of state administrators who were identified with the traditional and conservative group. Some changes in ICESA activities and opinions can be noted particularly in the discussions of the National Executive Committee meetings. While "conventional wisdom" about manpower programs may be debated, the tensions of recent years between the Manpower Administration and the ICESA resulted in part from lag or slower change in liberalization and perspective of manpower programs at the state levels. The changes in state administrators over the years, however, has made the ICESA more liberal.

Do ICESA officials and other state and federal employment security officials think that ICESA legislative activity was efficacious? The 1968 survey reported a high rating of ICESA legislative effectiveness. Almost ninety percent rated its influence and effectiveness in the top part of the scale. Interestingly, federal officials rated the influence of the ICESA greater than did state respondents.

Usefulness of the ICESA

In describing the ICESA, federal and state employment security officials indicated that it was most useful to them because it was informative (33 percent) or because it was a direct channel to state and federal officials (28 percent). Fewer indicated that it was useful to them because it resolved administrative problems (8 percent), resolved policy problems (9 percent), or influenced legislation (12 percent). There are also some interesting differences between the various groups of officials in their evaluation of ICESA activities. National officials rated ICESA usefulness as an informative device relatively low, while they indicated overwhelmingly that its usefulness was as a direct channel between state and federal officials. On the other hand, federal regional officials indicated that it was more useful as an informative device than as a direct channel. State administrators considered it as relatively less useful for information (while other state officials saw this as its main function) and more useful in influencing legislation. In general, all officials seemed to value its use as a communications bridge.

The very existence of the ICESA as an alternate channel and with an independent ability to act was an important influence on the Department of Labor and the Manpower Administration in their relationships with the states. Its existence induced close consideration of federal actions affecting the state agencies before they were taken, detered federal use of authoritative means, and served as a stimulus to cooperative methods. As one ICESA president noted:

> . . . its very existence has been a tremendous deterrent to those who would emasculate the role of the state agencies in this federal-state system of employment security.[20]

Without the ICESA, the relationship with the grant-financed individual state agencies might well have been quite different.

It is also important that the administrative group (state agencies) in this instance also was largely the interest group (ICESA). There was a natural carry-over between the roles. In many respects, the ICESA served as a bridge that helped to span the jurisdictional and political, as well as the administrative, gap. This bridge worked in both directions: the states were given a larger participatory role and access to decision making, and the federal government gained a relationship supplementary to the dichotomized hierarchical one. Since the membership of the ICESA was identical to the state half of the intergovernmental arrangement, 53 otherwise individual units were brought together with the federal level in an institutionalized and regularized device for cooperation and consultation.

CHAPTER III
FOOTNOTES

[1] Francis E. Rourke, <u>Intergovernmental Relations in Employment Security</u> (Minneapolis: University of Minnesota Press, 1952) pp. 112-13.

[2] ICESA, <u>Constitution</u> (1970), Art. IX.

[3] William Haber and Merrill G. Murray, <u>Unemployment Insurance in the American Economy: An Historical Review and Analysis</u> (Homewood, Illinois: Richard Irwin, 1966) p. 460.

[4] John Herling, "Aborting Federalism," <u>Washington Daily News</u>, July 26, 1966, p. 23.

[5] With respect to the Federal Advisory Council, see Joseph M. Becker, <u>Shared Government in Employment Security: A Study of Advisory Councils</u> (New York: Columbia University Press, 1959) p. 368.

[6] Rourke, <u>Intergovernmental Relations in Employment Security</u>, p. 78.

[7] Robert C. Goodwin, "Memorandum to Curtis Aller: Information for OEP on Federal-State Relations," July 26, 1967. The memorandum was in response to questions on intergovernmental relations by Farris Bryant of the Office of Emergency Planning, responsible at that time for federal-state relations.

[8]This plan was recommended for adoption by an academic symposium on aid for the unemployed. See Joseph M. Becker (ed.), In Aid of the Unemployed (Baltimore: Johns Hopkins Press, 1965) p. 294.

[9]See, for example, William Haber and Daniel H. Kruger, The Role of the United States Employment Service in a Changing Economy (Kalamazoo, Michigan: Upjohn Institute for Employment Research, 1964) pp. 59-97.

[10]Descriptive comments may be found in Haber and Murray, Unemployment Insurance, p. 457; and Herman Gray, Should State Unemployment Insurance be Federalized? (New York: American Enterprise Association, Inc., 1946) pp. 37-38. The functions of the committee and the different plans it operates are detailed in Interstate Conference of Employment Security Agencies, Committee on Interstate Benefit Payments, Guide to Authority and Responsibilities of the Interstate Benefit Payments Committee.

[11]See Haber and Murray, Unemployment Insurance, pp. 458-59.

[12]ICESA, Constitution (1968) p. 16.

[13]U.S. Congress, Senate Committee on Finance, Unemployment Insurance Amendments of 1966, Hearings, 88th Congress, 2nd Session (1966) pp. 143-45.

[14] U.S. Congress, House Committee on Ways and Means, *Unemployment Compensation*, 89th Congress, 2nd Session (1966). See comments in Haber and Murray, *Unemployment Insurance,* pp. 458-59.

[15] In one instance, many state administrators spent an entire month in Washington D.C., defeating proposals that tended to nationalize the program. See ICESA, *Annual Meeting* (1942) pp. 98-100.

[16] See ICESA, *Annual Meeting* (1960) p. 119; (1956) pp. 22-30; and (1952) pp. 58-64. Relationships with the ICESA often became strained when the labor official criticizing the ICESA in 1952 later became assistant secretary of Labor and Manpower Administrator.

[17] "A Job on the Jobless," *I.U.D. Digest* (Industrial Union Department, AFL-CIO), Vol. 3 (Summer 1958) pp. 10-19.

[18] Haber and Murray, *Unemployment Insurance*, pp. 458-59; see also ICESA, *Annual Meeting* (1956) p. 21.

[19] John Herling, "Aborting Federalism," *Washington Daily News*, July 26, 1966, p. 23.

[20] Eldred Hill of Virginia, ICESA, *Annual Meeting* (1965) p. 9.

4
Influence Relationships and ICESA Impact

Intergovernmental relationships, such as the federal-state employment security system, are formal and informal adaptations. Particularly important are adaptations in power and participation in the policy process. Since intergovernmental relationships are in a permanent state of development and imbalance, a focus on adaptation is often quite insightful.[1] In the employment security system, this perspective focuses on adaptations in the sharing of power, consequences for the participant organizations, and the type and form of this relationship. More specifically, it directs attention to the processes of absorbing additional elements into the decision making structure.

A key adaptive response, which has evolved over the years in the employment security system, is an extensive reciprocal influence arrangement. Each party receives various degrees of support, alliance, and cooperation from the other. Many informal, and a significant portion of the formal influence relationships functioned through the ICESA.

A useful distinction can often be drawn between formal and informal influence arrangements. Examples of both formal and informal sharing of the decision making power were readily apparent in the employment security system. Formal state relationships with the federal level, which involved the establishment of an openly avowed and formally ordered relationship, included ICESA committees, joint steering committees, the position and funding of the executive secretary, and the ICESA financial basis. Formal federal relationships with the states included the joint steering committees and federal consultants to ICESA committees. The ICESA generally provided the basis for these supplementary formal federal-state relationships. The executive secretary was especially important in this regard since he was a formal member of the top federal and ICESA policy levels.

The formal sharing of the decision making function was often the result of two factors. First, formal relationships are a response to the need to legitimize the authority of a governing group, win the consent of the governed, or establish stability of authority. It has been indicated that in formal arrangements, responsibility rather than power often is shared. Second, a formal relationship is a response to the administrative need to invite participation or to establish some form of self-government to assist in ordering the activities of a large organization. In this respect, formal relationships may serve as an orderly and reliable mechanism for reaching relevant groups. Unions, for example, can be effectively used by management in eliminating absenteeism and increasing efficiency. Applied to the employment security system, the ICESA served to help legitimize and communicate federal decisions and authority in some ways by consulting and participating in the formal decision making process without always materially affecting it. Formal cooperation may tend to provide the appearance rather than the substance of power.

The actual sharing of power may tend to operate in informal arrangements. This type of relationship is also well illustrated in the employment security system. For example, significant changes in the requirements for state agencies to purchase federal excess property were made through informal influence. It is likely that the policy on purchase of excess property would have been mandatory without the informal ICESA influence. While the distinction may be drawn that informal relationships tend to share power and formal relationships tend to share responsibility, the reverse may also be true. This and following chapters discuss the role of the ICESA and the influence, participation, and impact of those involved in the relationship.

ICESA Participation and Impact

What part was played by the Interstate Conference in the intergovernmental relationship? What impact did it have on the relationship of the state agencies and the federal level? Both federal and

TABLE 5

The Role of the ICESA in the 1968 Federal-State
Employment Security System

Questions	1	2	3	4	5	Mean
Relationship between BES and state agencies	Excellent 14%	67%	17%	Bad 2%	0%	2.07
Extent that relationship is a result of ICESA	Great 24	52	14	None 10	0	2.08
ICESA effect on state influence in system	Increases 14	65	19	Decreases 0	0	2.04

state employment security officials abstractly rated the general federal-state relationship in the 1968 employment security system as good, and perceived the ICESA to be responsible in large part for this relationship. The respondents indicated that the influence of the state agencies was increased by their participation in the ICESA. The ICESA was perceived to have actual access to and influence on the federal level and the employment security program.

One important factor to be considered in these ratings was the large number (61 percent) of Bureau of Employment Security officials who had experience in the employment security program at the state level. The relationship may have been good in part because many of the national BES officials had the background, perspectives, experience, and understanding of both the state and federal levels. Recruiting BES officials from the state level probably strengthened interlevel ties. One of the causes of tension in the 1969 reorganization was the placing of the employment security function under those who were not part of the traditional system. Thus, before the reorganization, the federal employment security agency was staffed in large part by system insiders responsive to state agency perspectives.[2] Both present and previous employment experiences of state and federal officials are important factors in perceptions and hence actions governed by those perceptions.

<u>Channels of Influence and the ICESA</u>

National and regional Manpower Administration offices and the ICESA were formal channels for state influence in the employment security program. Although the MA hierarchical channels seem quite responsive, the ICESA competed closely as a channel for state influence. The old Bureau of Employment Security, however, was somewhat more responsive as an object of state agency influence. The 1969 reorganization appears to have decreased total state influence both directly and through the ICESA.

In a comparison of the BES national and regional offices and the ICESA as effective channels for state influence, the 1968 survey ratings were very close. It is significant that the ICESA competed very closely with the BES regional and national offices as effective channels for actual state influence. It was perceived to be almost as important for state influence in the employment security program as the official relationships with the BES.[3]

It was also interesting that national and regional officials each thought that they were the most effective channel of influence for the state agencies. As a group, state administrators felt much more strongly than other respondents that the ICESA is effective as a channel for state influence. Those participating in ICESA activities perceived such activities to be most efficacious. Thus, each group of officials seemed to feel that the area of their own participation was somewhat more responsive.

Effectiveness of ICESA Officers

In this section the effectiveness of the various ICESA officers -- the ICESA president, the National Executive Committee (NEC), and the standing committees -- will be discussed. The president and the National Executive Committee were vehicles generally directed toward the concerns of state administrators. These two units were traditionally staffed by state administrators. The ICESA substantive committees probably served the purposes of the federal and lower level state officials to a greater extent. BES national officials felt that the committee activities, which focused largely on the administrative and smaller substantive issues, were more effective in advancing a constructive federal-state relationship than was the NEC, which focused on the political and larger program issues. The differing perceptions of the BES national officials and the state administrators were probably a reflection of the differing uses of the ICESA. Since the federal level generally controlled the initiation of policy, federal officials saw the constructive role of the

ICESA in the implementation and operation of policy (an administrative role), while state administrators saw the constructive role in the influence of policy (a political role).

Influence Points

In any system there are centers of institutional strength and power that make and enforce demands. At which points did the Interstate Conference have influence, and what were its relationships with each unit in the system? There were large differences in ICESA influence of the Congress, Department of Labor, Manpower Administration and its subunits, MA regions, and state agencies.

In general, the Interstate Conference appears to have had some influence and impact at all levels, particularly at the higher and lower levels. That is, the Congress and the second and third levels of the Manpower Administration appear to have been more responsive to Conference activities. The Department and Manpower Administration levels were much less responsive than the previous relationship with the Bureau of Employment Security. One reason that the 1969 reorganization was so bitterly fought was that those least responsive were being given larger formal roles over the employment security system.

The survey data taken before the reorganization clearly shows different degrees of influence and response. On the basis of these ratings, influence on Congress was rated slightly greater than parts of the more immediate system; the BES was also perceived to be very responsive to ICESA influence. In descending order, respondents felt that the ICESA had the most influence with the Congress, then the BES, the state agencies, the BES regions, the Department of Labor, and the Manpower Administration. The means fall within the categories of "very effective" for influence on Congress to "not very effective" with respect to the Manpower Administration.

Given the extent of ICESA influence, did the organizational units most influenced have the most control in the employment security system? The Assistant Secretary for Manpower and the Manpower Administrator are the most important with respect to the operation of the system, but they appear to be least influenced by ICESA activities. State and federal employment security officials in the 1968 survey perceived these levels to have relatively more control over the system than other levels. The state agencies (and the national BES) followed closely in the amount of perceived control; the regions and the Department of Labor levels appeared to have somewhat less control over what happens in the system.

The fragmentation of control among different organizational participants in the system creates for each participant the political role of gathering and giving support. It is probably this dispersion of power that afforded the ICESA such extensive access to decision making centers and enabled it to be effective at the different levels. The ICESA was in the important position of being able to lend support, legitimacy, and acceptance to the decisions and actions of other system participants. In particular, the organization of the

Manpower Administration prior to 1969, with its semi-autonomous and in many ways competitive BES, was a fruitful field for such support relationships. The ICESA and the state agencies were allied closely with the BES in this support relationship. Centralization of control in the reorganization of the Manpower Administration thus made the system less political and decreased ICESA effectiveness.

Participation and Control

To check observations about the extent of participation in the system, a control graph was constructed. Control graphs are descriptive models usually formed by participant perceptions of the control pattern in formal organizations.[4] The horizontal axis represents the hierarchical levels of an organization and the vertical axis represents the amount of control exercised by those levels. Two important analytical features of the control graph are the hierarchical distribution of control (the shape of the curve) and the total amount of control (the general height of the curve). For example, a curve that rises is autocratic; one that declines is democratic. A low flat curve represents a laissez-faire system and a high flat one represents a highly participative system.

In order to construct a control graph for the employment security system, federal and state officials were asked to rate the amount of control possessed by each level in the system. The results of the rating are presented in Figure 2.

FIGURE 2

Control Graph of the Employment Security System From 1968 Survey

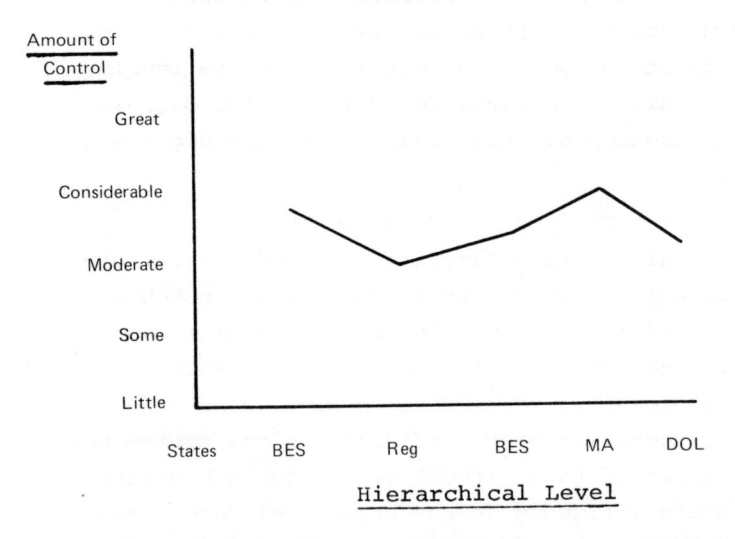

Amount of Control vs *Hierarchical Level* (States, BES, Reg, BES, MA, DOL); vertical axis levels: Little, Some, Moderate, Considerable, Great.

The graph indicates that each level has a significant amount of control within the system; the average height of the curve denotes moderate to considerable control. The total amount of control may be an important measure of organizational effectiveness and member attitudes; other studies have found a positive correlation between the amount of total control and the effective performance of an organization.[5] For example, a high degree of participation and control by each level may induce feelings of accomplishment, satisfaction, contribution, and ability to act. Thus, despite all of the frustrations and limitations of the system, the very fact that the employment security system was fragmented with each level having some control and power might have provided feelings of gratification, efficacy, and satisfaction to each level.

With respect to the distribution of control, the shape of the curve reflects the complex federal-state nature of the system. The curve has high points at both the federal and state levels; individually, the state agencies and the Manpower Administration had the highest relative degrees of control.

The ICESA and the System

The decision making function in the federal-state employment security system was shared through a variety of mechanisms. The state agencies had access and influence in multiple ways at the federal levels. The ICESA, in particular, significantly increased state influence in the system and was perceived to be almost as important a channel for state influence as the regular hierarchical, that is federal, channels. The ICESA was influential in gaining access to and influencing relevant legislative, administrative, and program centers. Power in the system was fragmented and a more political basis of operation was created. Centralization in recent reorganizations, however, decreased the political nature of the relationships. Even so, the employment security system was characterized by dispersion of power and high organizational participation by the various levels.

CHAPTER IV
FOOTNOTES

[1]Although not expressed in the same terminology, many of the author's concepts here are drawn from Philip Selznick's discussion of cooptation; see particularly his <u>TVA and the Grass Roots; A Study in the Sociology of Formal Organizations,</u> new preface (New York: Harper and Row, 1966).

[2]Measuring the significance of correlations in the cross-tabulations and contingency tables with Kendalls Tau, all officials clearly perceive the system in terms of their current and past work assignments. High Tau values were obtained in the cross-tabulation of state and federal experience with the various substantive responses.

[3]Although the means do not vary greatly, the ICESA ratings were more concentrated in the middle ranges of the scale while both the BES national and regional offices received more ratings at the extremities of the scale.

[4] See Arnold S. Tannenbaum and Robert L. Kahn, "Organizational Control Structure, A General Descriptive Technique as Applied to Four Local Unions," Human Relations, Vol. 10 (1957) pp. 127-140; Arnold S. Tannenbaum, "Control in Organizations: Individual Adjustment and Organizational Performance," Administrative Science Quarterly, Vol. 7 (September, 1962) pp. 236-57; Clagett G. Smith and Arnold S. Tannenbaum, "Organizational Control Structure; A Comparative Analysis," Human Relations, Vol. 16 (1963) pp. 299-316.

[5] Smith and Tannenbaum, "Organizational Control Structure," pp. 309, 313.

5
The Role of the ICESA: Operation and Evaluation

It is clear that the cooperative relationship in the employment security system was complex and that there were some extensive and significant associations between the state employment security agencies, units of the federal Department of Labor, the ICESA, and other participants in the system. This chapter discusses the operation of the employment security system with respect to the support relationships, the environment of decisions, aspects of formal control, factors of power sharing, tendencies toward independence and subordination, access to administrative controls, the pluralization of power, bridging the hierarchical gap, and other important factors in the operation of the ICESA.

The Function of Support

Cooperative relationships, where external organizations share in the decision making power or have some access to influencing policy, are more than expediencies. They generally exist because the groups involved each derive certain benefits from the relationship. One benefit given in return for either formal or informal access to decision centers is support or alliance for the group permitting access. The support of the ICESA, for example, was especially important for the BES in its relationships with Congress, the Department of Labor, and the Manpower Administration. In this respect, the ICESA was coopted by the BES as a source of support. The practical result of this access was that the two organizations often combined in efforts and gave support to the actions of the other.

Since each party in a reciprocal sharing-support relationship has some access to the decision making processes of the other, the relationship becomes suspect to some, especially competing groups. For this reason, the BES was criticized as a mere tool of the state agencies. While this disparaging description might have or might not have been true, there is no doubt that the state agencies did influence the BES through the ICESA. However, this relationship need not be seen in a negative light since the real meaning of terms like cooperation, consultation, cooperative or creative federalism, and participative or democratic administration essentially is the accommodation or influence of one unit with another.

These cooperative arrangements are certainly common in government. The merits of the specific substantive issues are a separate discussion, but the influence of one level on another need not be detrimental to any participant.

Support relationships vary by time and issue, but the frequent relationship with one group, the BES-ICESA relationship in this instance, often establishes general patterns and relationships that extend beyond specific issues and times. The patterns of continuing alliances of support may also create competing groups of other related organizations. The continuing relationship between the BES and the ICESA resulted in some dissatisfaction from competing units. The Department of Labor acknowledged in congressional testimony and statements that its relationships with the ICESA were not fully satisfactory.[1] ICESA support of the BES in departmental power struggles and over the direction of the program often created poor relationships with the department and Manpower Administration levels. In multiple attempts to reorganize the Manpower Administration and alter the internal power relationships, ICESA support through other channels, both formally and informally, was important to the BES. In an October 1968 reorganization attempt, the Secretary of Labor issued a reorganization _fait_ _accompli_ without prior announcement or consultation with affected parties. This quick action was probably designed in part to minimize ICESA intercession in support of the Bureau. The importance of the BES-ICESA relationship for the

BES was also illustrated by the fact that one of the first acts of the reorganization was the immediate relocation of an important coordinator of BES-state support, the ICESA executive secretary. Within hours, the executive secretary was isolated both organizationally and physically from the Bureau and placed near the manpower administrator. Through formal positions and informal contacts with governors, congressmen, other groups, and individuals including the President of the United States, Secretary Willard Wirtz was ultimately forced to suspend the reorganization. The subsequent sucessful reorganization by Secretary George Shultz in the new administration was probably successful in part due to the careful consultation and clearance to get the support of all interested parties including the ICESA. Secretary Shultz and Assistant Secretary for Manpower Arnold Weber met at least four times with ICESA committees on this internal reorganization of the Department of Labor. ICESA activities and suggestions in this process generally supported positions favorable both to the BES and the state agencies. One important state interest, of course, was to maintain the Bureau with which they had generally satisfactory relationships and an established alliance.

An extensive mutual support identification, however, can be disadvantageous. One reason, for example, why an important program was not assigned to the BES at the national level -- although the BES had prepared for the program -- was that the BES was considered to have been coopted by the states. The Work Incentive Program of the 1967

Social Security amendments was not assigned to the BES, one official told the author, because departmental officials felt it would not sufficiently prod or push the states. In this instance, the close relationship precluded confidence that the BES would work with the states in the manner desired. Whether the program would have worked better through the cooperative BES relationship or through another bureau not coopted by the state agencies remained a source of discussion among program participants until the reorganization in 1969.

Although mutual support between groups tends to be discussed in cooperative terms, it should be recognized that the relationship also reflects a state of tension between the two groups.[2] In fact, tension in the system may be a cause of the relationship, which, once established, may tend to appease the points of actual or potential opposition and lead to the extension of the support relationship. The federal system, especially the federal-state employment security system, is based in tension since separate power centers create a need for some kind of mechanism through which the parts can effectively relate.

The ICESA in a Tension Relationship

Although mutual support between groups tends to be discussed in cooperative terms, it should be recognized that the relationship also reflects a state of tension between the two groups.[2] In fact, tension in the system may be one cause of the relationship which, once established, may tend to appease the points of actual or potential opposition and lead to the extension of the support relationship. The federal system, especially in the employment security, is based in tension since separate power centers create a need for some kind of relationship through which the parts can effectively relate.

Probably the largest source of tension between the Manpower Administration and the Interstate Conference is the increasingly competetive program and financial structure of the manpower effort in the United States. After the early 1960's, fiscal sources, organizational structures, and manpower programs proliferated to radically influence the relationships in the traditional employment security program. When only Title III funds of the Social Security Act were available, the question was largely the allocation of one source of money to one set of recipients in one general program. The addition of MDTA, Economic Opportunity Act, and other programs with their separate fiscal sources and organizational structures reduced the relative status and power of the ICESA. With this change in manpower programs, the overall coverage and impact of the Interstate Conference has decreased.

Many other competitive units have entered the manpower arena in recent years. Business, labor, Urban Leagues, private non-profit groups, Community Action Associations, and other groups are competing for manpower program funds. Many programs have directly involved the mayors and local agencies rather than mayors are taking a larger role in manpower planning and programs. Many programs have directly involved the mayors and local agencies rather than dealing through the state agencies. These changes have also reduced the relative role of the ICESA and have induced competition and tension in the MA-ICESA relationship.

Tensions are also increased by the different manpower program perspectives of the Manpower Administration and the Interstate Conference. There have been long and tense discussions over the organization and operation of the Manpower Administration, for example, when the Assistant Secretary for Manpower or the Manpower Administrator have appeared before the ICESA National Executive Committee meetings. The ICESA has been vocal and active with respect to the design, operation, and assignment of manpower programs and even with respect to the internal organization and operation of the Manpower Administration.

The Manpower Administration and its superiors are in the role of monitoring and insuring performance without being directly over the performing organizations. The national government is quite vulnerable to pressures from Congress, minorities, and other national groups. This puts the national government in the tension creating role of generating furter pressures on the state agencies to perform more effectively.

All in all, the competitive and fragmented manpower system in the United States creates some natural tensions between the ICESA, the state agencies, and the Manpower Administration.

Control: The Sharing of Power and Responsibility
To discuss control and control attempts in the

federal-state employment security system, it is useful to divide the control process into three different aspects: the substantive phase concerned with basic policy or program decision making, the procedural phase concerned with day-to-day organizational expediting, and the sanctions phase or the punishment of nonconformity. In both formal and informal arrangements there is sharing of power and responsibility in the employment security system.

Formal Relationships

Formal relationships seem to share power in both substantive and procedural areas. There are many good illustrations of actual influence through formal devices. The 1967-68 Urban Affairs Committee was able to achieve a significant policy modification in the designation of the state agencies as the deliverer of manpower services rather than as a "presumptive deliverer" in the Title I-B Economic Opportunity Act programs delegated to the Department of Labor. The activities of the Work Incentive Program Committee in 1968, as described earlier, also illustrate the actual sharing of power through formal devices. In the procedural or administrative phase, various federal-ICESA joint steering committees shared power in the design, development, and implementation of an automatic data processing system, staff training and development, and management improvement activities.

Formal relationships share responsibility as well as power; they legitimize decisions as well as influence them. Many substantive and procedural items, for example, are discussed in ICESA committee meetings at the request of federal participants with the intent to gain acceptance of the state agencies, to transmit information, and to be able to say that consultation has taken place. This is well-illustrated by committee discussions of procedural matters such as fiscal decisions and personnel specifications, and discussions of substantive matters such as various programs and policies. In fact, the agendas of most ICESA committees were largely taken up with this sort of discussion.

Informal Relationships

In informal relationships, actual influence or sharing of control is extensive but often difficult to document. In addition, it is difficult to determine to what extent state officials were acting as individuals or using the ICESA framework. Many of those intervirewed noted the importance of the ICESA as a basis for officials to informally contact congressional, federal, and other state people. Some of the most effective influence attempts in both substantive and procedural areas were informal in nature. Substantive legislative matters, for example, were effectively influenced through informal contacts. The state agencies' efforts in blocking the October 1968 reorganization were in large part informal and covert contacts with governors, congressmen, the President, and other influential persons.

Informal sharing of responsibility is even more difficult to discern; however, it appears that responsibility was shared internally and that decisions were legitimized in the reciprocal support relationships of these participating groups. Acceptance of decisions, of course, is one of the objectives of an informal relationship; responsibility in the form of indebtedness is generally shared informally rather than overtly. In some instances, responsibility and legitimization are spread informally to external cooperating groups through further influence or support relationships. For example, the bargaining and influence with respect to the legislative proposal for phased-in quarterly collections of the Federal Unemployment Tax and the 1969 reorganization created internal acceptance and indebtedness as a result of cooperation and support. This covert and informal relationship was then extended to other groups, such as the Unemployment Benefit Advisers when they participated in tangent support relationships with any of the participants.

Formal Sanctions

The third category into which control processes were arbitrarily divided was the sanction phase or the punishment of nonconformity. The extreme nature of the formal sanctions that were available to the Department of Labor (withholding all funds and finding a state out-of-conformity) precluded their use except in extreme and rare instances. Since these sanctions were rarely used and were confined to specific states and specific issues, the states seldom combined through the ICESA for action or influence. The ICESA investigated conformity questions, but apparently did not feel the need to be concerned with this area in recent years. The conformity questions, for example, that arose from the proposed reorganization of the state agency by the 1968 California legislature did **not** become an issue within the ICESA. When ICESA action was taken, obviously, it was focused toward sharing power rather than legitimizing the decision or sharing responsibility for it.

The Environment of Decisions

Instead of the atomistic approaches of separate units to specific issues, the ICESA created an overall, regularized, continuing environment. This relationship itself was important to actions within the system; stated more precisely, the environment influenced the decision centers. Thus, influence attempts could be effectively directed at the environment without trying to force specific decision makers and without attempting to assume the decision making authority. Indirect environmental pressures could yield the same results, and were often more acceptable to those involved than was direct action. The continuance of the overall association produced an additional tendency to maintain the best possible relationship even at the expense of some specific interests and actions. Although conflict was not precluded, there was a tendency toward a cooperative relationship since both parties were interested in maintaining the overall association.

Also, the ICESA provided a rational environment for both federal and state activities, an environment and role within which certain federal and state agency behavior patterns were more acceptable and rational. For example, state agency lobbying activities by **an** intermediate organization were more acceptable to general state governments and Congress. A rational basis for joint action toward all states was provided for the federal level, eliminating the need to deal with each state individually. Especially important, it provided a rationale of representation in which a few state officials could represent many. The ICESA also helped to communicate expectations, needs, feelings, rationales, and predilections within the system, enabling participants to relate to the system and to act rationally within it. The ICESA Executive Secretary, privy to the top policy levels of both the federal level and the ICESA and an important communicator for each, was especially important in this regard.

Factors of Power Sharing

A major determinant in the sharing of power was the degree of willingness on the federal level, which possessed more devices of control and power. The federal level, of course, also benefited from the relationship, and it may have been an effective way, from their standpoint, of relating to the state agencies. Even so, this relationship existed largely because of their willingness to finance it and to share access to their decision centers. The personal willingness of the BES administrator to cooperate in this fashion was very important to the relationship and its development over the past twenty years, a tendency that ICESA presidents have appreciated.[3] The same degree of cooperation, or in effect power sharing, has not been present since the reorganization; the relationship is maintained on a formal basis.

The relative balance of power between the

federal and state levels was also significant to the sharing of power and the access to decision centers. The relationship in the employment security system was not one of a government agency and private interest groups, but one of two government levels, both possessing areas of power, decision, and responsiblity. Thus, there was an important trade-off for participation not found to this extent in relationships with private groups; each had an important official area of decision and leadership to which access, consultation, and cooperation could be given in exchange for reciprocal access, consultation, and cooperation. In this respect, the BES was coopted by the state agencies, and the state agencies were coopted by the BES. Indeed, the administrative and political separation between the state agencies and the federal government served to enhance the relationship in some ways by creating a balance between the two power centers.

Tendencies Toward Independence and Subordination

Cooperative arrangements between organizations can promote either subordination and dependence, or independence and freedom of action. In this respect the relationship between the state agencies and the federal level in the employment security system was important to the future of each organizational participant. In 1955 the Commission on Intergovernmental Relations noted:

> To be sure, there is a risk that the State participation in joint schemes, while bolstering the

> States as going organizations,
> may induce habits of subordina-
> tion and deference to external
> initiative and guidance. In the
> long run this risk is less serious
> for the States than the effects of
> being bypassed.[4]

In the ICESA relationship, habits appeared to be those of cooperation and sharing of decision making rather than subordination and deference; the formal relationship of the two levels, however, may have tended in the other direction. As an institutionalized third party, the ICESA permitted the state agencies and the federal partner to meet on a more equal ground for the resolution of issues. Individual state agencies would not have been as effective in their separate relationships because the ICESA had a wider possiblity of action alternatives, combined atomistic state units for a more equal power balance, had a national-state viewpoint and interest, was recognized as a cooperative discussion ground separated from program and operational ties, and was an institutionalized and continuing relationship.

At the same time, neither the state agencies nor the federal level needed to share power out of magnanimity since each received important returns from participation. For the federal level it was simply an effective way to handle the difficult federal-state relationship. For example, some theorized that the more the national officials used nonauthoritative methods and the more state officials participated in the decision making process, the more cooperative the federal-state relationship would be, the less likely the chance that the program would be altered against the wishes of national administrators, and the greater the probability that the values of the national administrators would be implemented in the long run.[5]

It may be that cooperation reinforced rather than reduced the structural integrity of the federal system. One student of federalism believed, for example, that the states preserved their integrity not through a sharp separation from the national level but within an intricate framework of cooperative relationships that maintain their structural integrity while tying all levels together functionally in a common task of service.[6] Another wrote that the vitality of functional union made federalism workable.[7] In a speech to the ICESA, Frank Bane, former executive director of the Council of State Governments, said that the federal system is maintained in part by the development of interstate cooperation and the facilitation of federal-state relationships.[8]

Access to Administrative Controls

The ICESA, through the work of its committees, was particularly well-suited to influence the horizontal coordinative services such as budget, planning, and personnel controls. Since these important administrative controls were largely federal in nature, it is significant that the ICESA participated closely with federal officials in their explanation, discussion, formulation, and modification. ICESA committees reviewed sixteen or so specific areas in detail with federal personnel responsible for these areas. The continuing nature of this relationship and the knowledge that any action might require

levels were forced to seek support where they could find it. In this respect, the ICESA was important as a source, receiver, and facilitator of support.

Second, on the basis of shared attitudes, claims were made between the groups for the establishment, maintenance, or enhancement of behavior implied by the shared attitudes.[9] In spite of various disagreements on details, the basic desire for an effective employment security and manpower program bound the participants and groups together within the same general system, provided the basis for demands, gave the rationale for positions and philosophies, and helped to legitimize actions. This commonly shared desire for the effectiveness of the system acted to legitimize the various, and often opposing, positions and actions of the various groups and enabled them to relate to each other on a common basis.

Third, ICESA membership was identical to the state agencies and in many ways was an alter-ego through which the state agencies performed functions not otherwise possible. The boundaries of other groups interested in the employment security system were generally more indefinite and overlapping. All ICESA members were state agency officials who participated as officials from their respective state governments. Membership in the ICESA was thus more formal and restricted than the membership of other interested groups. The limited scope and semi-official nature of ICESA membership enhanced its internal cohesiveness and the closeness of its relationship to the federal government.

Fourth, the relationships and roles of indi-

discussion and explanation at the discretion of the state representatives tended to reduce arbitrary federal decisions.

Pluralization of Power

Basic to the federal principle is the view that power should be plural rather than centralized. As a supplement to the regular hierarchical relationship, the ICESA served in part to disperse power, as well as to increase state power. This might have made the federal system more competitive and in a sense the dispersal of power into multiple official, semi-official, and nonofficial units in the federal system might have supplemented the traditional geographical dispersion of power. Certainly, it made it more difficult for one level, especially the federal partner, to take unilateral action toward direction or modification of the system. One may legitimately disagree with the policy that resulted from this system while accepting the process that is characteristic of the American democratic system of checks and balances and dispersion of power. A balance between an emphasis on policy and a focus on process necessitates being aware of the benefits of each and minimizing their disadvantages.

Factors of Group Interaction

A number of factors influenced and shaped the operation of the ICESA in the employment security system from the perspective of group relationships. As noted above, the system operated on a mutual support relationship. The need for support forced the administrator to play a political role and to be responsive to other levels and groups. The administrators at both the state and national

viduals in the various tangent and participant groups tended to be stabilized through the group relationships. The ICESA provided an institutionalized relationship that enabled a much broader and more stable range of roles and action alternatives for all participants. State officials, in addition, were provided with continuing roles and offices through which they could act as representatives of the states at large.

Fifth, the relationship between the ICESA and the federal government, was contingent and precarious to the extent that each had a different basis of action and interest. In spite of the shared attitudes noted above, conflict and tension often resulted from the fact that the ICESA and the Department of Labor operated from separate viewpoints. Tension and conflict seemed to have been created more by actions predicated on political bases than those predicated on administrative bases, and, accordingly, the units had more in common with respect to the administrative than the political basis. Administrative actions were more acceptable within the system than political actions; actions with respect to the implementation of the program found less criticism than actions with respect to legislation. Insofar as the bases of action differed, the relationship was more critical and contingent.

Sixth, the development of the relationship and the relationship itself were based on an evolutionary rather than revolutionary process. The ICESA -- both in an organizational and operational sense -- evolved gradually without a fully preconceived design. Created with the support and financial assistance of the federal government, the ICESA developed into a much different and more extensive force than was originally envisioned. Once securely established, the ICESA was able to expand upon that basis and extend its influence and activities.

Seventh, the formal organization of the group was an important factor in the survival and influence of the ICESA. The financing, the location of the Executive Secretary in the top ICESA and federal policy levels, the extensive relationships through the committee structure, and the National Executive Committee were very important to the relative ICESA success and limitations as an organization.

Eighth, although consultative processes and representation of interests were largely accepted with respect to the ICESA, the system as a whole and in its parts had to remain responsive to other forces. It was not a closed system. Although the old BES was responsive to the ICESA, this relationship and source of support was not sufficient for either the state agencies or the BES. The units of the system had to relate in concert and separately to Congress, the Department of Labor, other government units, and important outside groups.

Maintenance of the Relationship

One of the problems facing any organizational relationship is the difficulty of maintaining vitality and effective performance. Philip Selznick observed that an important organizational problem of democracy in general is the maintenance of democratic or cooperative relationships since democratic participation tends to break down into administrative involvement.[10] He noted that this is not a matter of the morals or goodwill of the agents in the relationship but is an organizational tendency and problem. Likewise, it was difficult for the Interstate Conference to maintain the vitality and efficacy of the relationship between the ICESA and the federal and state agencies. Committee meetings often tended to become detailed administrative discussions at the expense of real policy or operational achievements. Committee members complained that these meetings often consisted largely of routine federal recitations and presentations to a somewhat captive audience. An ICESA president was disturbed that "all too often our federal partner makes declarations to our committees and then calls it consultation."[11]

Changes in administrations and departmental reorganizations created problems in developing and maintaining the relationship. Changes in Presidents and cabinet officers, however, permitted the relationship to erase some old contentions and start with a new slate. This often was to the advantage of the continuing parties such as the ICESA and the old BES. The 1968-69 reorganizations of the Manpower Administration, however, were partly a conflict over the maintenance and course of the relationship. Even though the formal organizational relationship with the ICESA was retained, tensions were created and the level of involvement quite naturally receded to the simpler formal relationships.

CHAPTER V
FOOTNOTES

[1] See U.S. Congress, Senate Subcommittee on Intergovernmental Relations of the Committee on Government Operations, *Creative Federalism*, 90th Congress, 1st Session (1967), p. 247 for the prepared statement of the Secretary of Labor and pp. 238-39 for his oral testimony.

[2] See Philip Selznick, *TVA and the Grass Roots; A Study in the Sociology of Formal Organization*, (New York: Harper and Row, 1966) p. 217; and Philip Selznick, "Foundations of the Theory of Organization," *American Sociological Review*, Vol. 13 (February, 1948) p. 35.

[3] See for example, ICESA, *Annual Meeting*, (1966) pp.7, 47; (1964) p. 8; (1960) p. 9; and (1958) p. 32. Shortly after his appointment over twenty years ago, the BES administrator commented on his intent to cooperate that "the Federals have been inclined to look on a successful federal-state relationship as one where they came out with most of the things that they wanted and the State people have been inclined to do the same thing. Actually, a successful federal-state relationship, in my opinion -- it is judged by whether or not there is a real give and take, a real development of community of interest, and a working together to solve common problems." ICESA, *Annual Meeting*, (1948) p. 21.

[4] U.S. Commission on Intergovernmental Relations, A Report to the President for Transmittal to the Congress, (1955) p. 67.

[5] Edward W. Weidner, Intergovernmental Relations as Seen by Public Officials (Minneapolis: University of Minnesota Press, 1960) p. 254.

[6] Daniel J. Elazar, American Federalism: A View from the States (New York: Thomas Y. Crowell, 1966) pp. 1-2.

[7] Arthur W. Macmahon, "The Problems of Federalism: A Survey," in Federalism: Mature and Emergent, ed. Arthur W. Macmahon (Garden City, New York: Doubleday, 1955) p. 22.

[8] ICESA, Annual Meeting (1949) p. 85.

[9] Essentially, this is Truman's definition of an interest group. See David B. Truman, The Governmental Process; Political Interests and Public Opinion (New York: Knopf, 1953) p. 33.

[10] Selznick, TVA and the Grass Roots, p. 265.

[11] ICESA, Annual Meeting (1966) p. 7.

6
Intergovernmental Relations in Employment Security

The interdependent and complex nature of the relationship between the federal and state employment security agencies often created difficulties in establishing and maintaining effective employment service and unemployment insurance systems. Satisfactory administrative processes and policy relationships were difficult where the federal and state governments shared power and responsibility. The federal system severed what would otherwise be regular hierarchical relationships in the employment security system and thus intensified many system needs. The organizational need, for example, for program design and direction was complex in the employment security program where control was shared by two separate and independent jurisdictions

Complementary Relationships

The general needs of federal-state systems can be seen as both administrative and political. The administrative needs include the needs to coordinate, integrate, and communicate. Political needs include the needs to influence, legitimize, and share power and responsibility. The bifurcated federal-state system often makes it difficult for the administrative and political needs of the system and its participants to be met.

Some approaches and techniques to meet these system needs were investigated in the federal-state employment security system. An extra-hierarchical organization of state agencies was found to be important in a variety of respects in the operation of the intergovernmental process. The functions of the Interstate Conference of Employment Security Agencies have been illustrated in the intergovernmental relationship between the state employment security agencies, the former Bureau of Employment Security, and, to some extent, the Manpower Administration.

The ICESA was shown to have an important impact in providing mutual access to decision centers and facilitating the sharing of power. Although the employment security system had substantial federal controls, there was a significant dispersion of power resulting partly from the activities of the Interstate Conference. State influence was increased through participation in the ICESA. Indeed, the ICESA was seen by system participants to be almost as important a channel for the state agencies to influence the employment security program as were the regular regional and national channels. The ICESA also performed many procedural and coordinative functions for the state agencies and the federal government.

The ICESA helped to fill both political and administrative needs of the system in its functions as a direct channel for consultation, a collective state voice, a cooperative mechanism, and an influence agent on policy and legislation. It also functioned as a process for technical review and comment, a cooperative management device, an interstate agent performing functions outside the control and responsibility of either the individual state or federal governments, and a medium of interstate and intergovernmental communication. Specifically, many administrative needs of the federal-state employment security system were met because the ICESA functioned as a supplementary communication channel, coordinating agent, and integrating device for the federal and various state jurisdictions. Some of the political needs of the system were met as the ICESA provided a means for the various actors to relate to one another, influence and be influenced, legitimize, and share power and responsibility.

Putting aside the substantive impact and the program consequences of ICESA influence on policy in the employment security program, the ICESA made important procedural contributions to the operation of the system. It was important as a supplementary process facilitating the operation of the federal-state employment security system through providing formal and informal access to decision centers and meeting some of the administrative and political needs for both the state employment security agencies and the federal government. In this respect it was a useful supplementary relationship between the federal and state governments.

Efficacy and Impact of Participation

Each organizational unit in the employment security system influenced and was influenced by the other units in the relationship, and each operated within the give and take of the system. The advantages and disadvantages of this relationship for each system unit were important to the overall operation and success of the relationship. This section examines the efficacy of the relationship for the federal and state agencies.

The Federal Level

It is clear from the public commitments to cooperate and the activities described in the foregoing chapters that the federal level cooperated willingly with the ICESA and the state agencies in many ways. This willingness to cooperate probably derived in part from the benefits that the federal level received from the relationship. At the same time, the relationship was in many ways neither the creation of nor to the liking of the federal level.

From the national viewpoint, the relationship with the ICESA was useful because it provided a direct channel to the state officials, was informative, helped to resolve policy and administrative problems, and assisted in influencing beneficial legislation. As a communication device, the ICESA was an available, convenient, quick, and effective way for the federal level to resolve differences, establish state positions, and promote federal objectives without dealing with fifty separate jurisdictions. It brought state and federal people together in an open forum for discussion, development of personal contacts and relationships, and exchange of information and viewpoints.

The ICESA relationship also served the federal level as a sounding board representing the operating level. This may have helped to avoid pitfalls while providing some guidance on the value and feasibility of policies and programs. Officially recognizing this function, the BES reported to the Federal Advisory Council in 1955 that "the Bureau uses this machinery [ICESA] as a device for securing State consultation on various program matters, usually while the program activity is in the planning stage."[1] It was helpful to the federal level in the development, installation, and continuing operation of programs, for example, in the management improvement and automation area. Although often in oppositon, the ICESA was also useful to the federal level as a support in legislative and other political matters, particularly as a political channel to state agencies, congressmen, governors, and other groups.

The ICESA was also beneficial to the federal level as a convenient method for influencing the perspectives and positions of various states. Some of the weaker state administrators were influenced positively by ICESA activity, and the ICESA helped to gain state acceptance of policies. One reply to the Rourke questionnaire in the early fifties noted:

> The Interstate Conference committees on various aspects of the program have been quite educational to the state administrators. It has been a good vehicle for giving the state agencies Bureau technical thinking through a medium which is often more acceptable

to some of the state administrators than the Bureau itself.[2]

At the same time, the Interstate Conference can impede and oppose through all of the above functions. The ICESA, in fact, has a reputation of active opposition. The difficulty is that what one person viewed as obstruction might have been viewed as the redemption of the employment security program by another. The ICESA tended to represent certain ideological positions, but then so did the other units in the relationship, including the Manpower Administration. As in most philosophical differences, each could produce warrants and logic to substantiate its position. The ICESA was at first employer-oriented and some state administrators have not agreed with redirection of the program toward the disadvantaged segments of the population. There appear, however, to have been significant changes over the years in the ICESA. With the normal turnover in state administrators and the resulting change in the National Executive Committee there was a growing acceptance of manpower innovations and a more liberal ICESA position. Still, the Interstate Conference tended to be more conservative and state-oriented while the Manpower Administration tended to be more liberal and nationally-oriented. This is the basis for what was probably the most serious claim against the Interstate Conference: that the ICESA impeded progress in the employment security system, a system that many had criticized for its lack of progress.

A related complaint was that the Interstate Conference restricted the rightful program and management function of the U.S. Department of

Labor, particularly the Manpower Administration. There was some substance to this complaint. For example, the hierarchically subordinate BES was able, through ICESA support, to oppose the Manpower Administration quite successfully in matters ranging from policy to internal management. In close cooperation with the ICESA, the Bureau was even able, in effect, to nullify the reorganization issued by Secretary Willard Wirtz. While having large responsibilities and feeling the need to significantly change the nation's manpower programs, the Manpower Administration has functioned in a difficult position for a supervisory organization: it was separated from the operational level; the subordinate units for most of its existence were semi-autonomous and often politically more powerful; and its actions were limited by the important and often opposing influence of an interest group in combination with the operational level (state agencies), the subordinates (BES), and some of the superiors (Congress and the President). Obviously, traditional management control functions could not operate effectively in such an environment, and the authority and the responsibility of the Manpower Administration was thus limited.

While the claim that the management functions of the Manpower Administration were impeded is valid, there are two opposing perspectives that should be recognized. First, managerial authority does not automatically or inherently reside at the top of an organization. Although some may argue for an inherent right to command, actual authority or power rests on consent and acceptance by the governed.[3] The theory that a bureaucracy is an integrated unit which operates as a neutral instrument and is controlled by authority residing at the top is inaccurate as a description and unattainable as an ideal. A bureaucracy is a human organization, not a machine, and it operates as part of a system where power is highly fragmented and there is participative policy-making and political influence. It is recognized, however, that traditional authority and political operation must be balanced. Political actions are to be expected, in fact are induced, in this kind of a system. If the ICESA had fragmented managerial control to the extent that program effectiveness, coordination, and performance were seriously impeded, then the ICESA would not have been beneficial to the system. The case can be made, however, that while the ICESA opposed the Manpower Administration in many particulars, it did help to bridge the federal-state gap and improve communication, coordination, program effectiveness, and so forth.

The second point is relevant in resolving the first. The argument that the ICESA seriously impeded the managerial capacity of the Manpower Administration should deal with concepts from participative management and democratic administration. Particularly since valid claims can be made for a voice and role in the system for the state agencies, a cooperative and more open style of management is appropriate. In a democracy, participation may be an added control and check. Some have argued that a more responsible bureaucracy is one that operates through pluralistic competition of policy alternatives and perspectives. The assumption is that policy is improved when submitted to critical discussion. While Interstate Conference activities may have resulted in policies that particular individuals oppose, benefits often result from open and competitive policy and program structures.

The State Employment Security Agencies

The state employment security agencies received many of the same benefits from the ICESA as did the federal level. These included use of the ICESA as a means of federal-state and state-state communication; as a collective state agent for concerted action, national representation, and unification for influence and action; and in negotiation as a recognized spokesman. The ICESA provided a mechanism and rationale for states to meet, establish common state positions, and take coordinated action. And, in some respects, the ICESA-state agency relationship helped some states to "lift their sights," better understand national objectives, develop views broader than single state interests, and make new programs and activities more acceptable through state participation in their development.

While the ICESA was useful for most states in influencing the operation of the employment security system and related legislation, it was probably more useful in this respect for the smaller states than the larger ones. The smaller states tended to have a proportionally larger voice in the activities of the Interstate Conference.

While the state employment security agencies benefited greatly from the activities of the ICESA, observations indicate that most of the gains were in the area of processes rather than substantive or policy ends. Although most criticism was directed at the substantive ends fostered by the ICESA and although these were often the most visible activities to outsiders, much of the impact of the relationship is in the area of administrative coordination and communication.

The Interstate Conference

The Interstate Conference, in many respects, was a proxy for the state agencies rather than a separate organization interested in separate ends. To most federal and state employment security officials in the 1968 survey, the ICESA was either considered as synonomous with the state agencies or as a process or catalyst not benefiting by itself. In the view of the participants, the ICESA appeared to be a "means" rather than an "ends" organization.

With respect to degree of impact, the role of the ICESA in the employment security program decreased after the 1969 reorganization. This is probably due, first, to the severance and attempted reestablishment of the relationship with the ICESA, and, second, to the fact that, while ICESA interests were identical with the old Bureau of Employment Security, they were only a portion of the concern of the Manpower Administration. Third, the philosophy of the Manpower Administration in many respects countered the past policy positions of the ICESA and the BES.

It is interesting that federal officials in the survey assessed ICESA impact and achievement of objectives as higher than did state officials, who generally indicated only limited or moderate success. State officials were more ambitious and abstract in defining ICESA goals,[4] but felt that only limited progress has been made toward these ends. Federal officials defined ICESA purposes in state-serving terms and felt that they were being accomplished generally.

Many of the ICESA successes are attributable to the activities of Conference officers, including the executive secretary, and to its ability to influence important power centers outside the U.S. Department of Labor, especially political power centers in Congress and the states. At the same time, internal factions prevented the ICESA from being more effective; liberal-conservative, labor-management, and large-small state divisions seriously hindered Conference unity and goal consensus. Negative aspects of past positions and support of the BES in internal federal struggles carried over into the relationship with the Manpower Administration.

Some factors commonly suggested as serious ICESA limitations include inadequate representation of states in the ICESA; its domination by conservative state administrators; influence of employer groups, especially the Unemployment Benefit Advisers; narrow outlook; reluctance to make changes and be responsive to new programs and needs; and a tendency to conserve rather than to innovate. Some complain that the ICESA meddled in federal agency politics, such as Department of Labor organizational problems.

Changes generally suggested for the ICESA included improvements in organizational structure, the image of the Conference, relationships with the U.S. Department of Labor, and ideological positions. Others proposed stronger leadership, changes in the controlling power structure, abolishing the informal rotation of offices, and creating an independent financial basis. Committees, it was suggested, should have more continuity, two-year staggered terms, longer meetings, independent staff assistance, and a heavier program rather than administrative composition. Suggestions to improve the office of executive secretary included additional staff, an independent location, and separate financing. It was also suggested that an additional officer be added for full-time congressional liaison. Several proposed changes in state representation in ICESA activities included the following: weighted voting by workers and employers covered by unemployment insurance rather than equal state votes; more voice and participation for unemployment insurance and employment service directors, including voting privileges rather than the extensive control and participation by state administrators; less domination by the smaller states; more regions for wider participation; and a reduction in the number of committee members for more effective committees.

It is interesting that many of the changes that were suggested to improve the ICESA dealt with internal matters within the capability of the states themselves. The one critical exception, of course, was the relationship with the Manpower Administration and the U.S. Department of Labor, and which was only partially within the capacities of the states.

The ICESA appears to have been a needed buffer zone which performed mechanistic and procedural functions in a supplementary relationship. High mutual influence was beneficial in many ways to the effective operation, coordination, and integration of the employment security system. Even though the ICESA performed many useful functions in the system, grounds for criticism and dissatisfaction also existed. Philosophical and policy differences are important evaluations. On this basis, some vigorously defend and some vigorously castigate the Interstate Conference. The procedural benefits of the ICESA and the desirability of meaningfully involving the state agencies probably outweighed some specific policies that might have resulted. Although certain ends were favored, the ICESA relationship was used to support and obtain acceptance of a variety of ends. As has been illustrated, the ICESA worked both ways: the state agencies influenced the federal government, while the federal level influenced the states for their purposes. Accepting the assumption that the states should have an effective voice in the federal-state employment security system, the democratic analogy can be drawn that participative systems are desirable even though one may disagree at times with specific candidates or policies that result from the system.

State Roles in the Federal System

One of the most important areas for assessment and evaluation of the Interstate Conference is the impact on the federal-state relationship. Much conventional wisdom about general federal-state relationships holds that there is federal control and state subordination.[5] A related contention is that the states are becoming administrative extensions of the federal government and declining as separate political entities.[6] Other variations of these common concerns about the changing role and impact of the states include the flow of power from the states to the national level, federal ascendancy through national initiative and control, and the acceleration of these trends through grant relationships.[7] It is often maintained that the growth of federal activities has served to break down the traditional division of power, decrease the role of the states, and limit their prerogatives. States are forced, some say, into this subordinate position through federal programs that are not refusable politically and financially.[8] Concern over the shift of power to the federal level is not an uncommon perspective, and the strengthening of state powers is a common prescription.[9]

In the employment security system, the states appear to have been subordinate administrative extensions and the federal government appears to have controlled the powerful directive functions when analyzing formal, overt procedures. The states, however, have substantial impact and control through other, generally less visible, means. The common focus on functional responsibilities, formal activities, and legal relationships is an inadequate basis for understanding relationships and roles in the federal-state system. Other dimensions of the relationship discussed in this study -- cooperative arrangements, informal processes, extra-hierarchical groups, and supplementary political relationships -- must be considered before adequate conclusions can be drawn about the role of the states and their impact and function in the system.

Although the state role may be redefined, the role of cooperation, influence, and power sharing need not be a less effective role. Indeed, states might be more effective in this role than in challenging and reversing the formal distribution of functions -- a struggle in which the federal government appears to have the advantage.

Formally centralized power may be shared in a variety of informal relationships. For example, the BES-ICESA-state agency relationship served to decentralize and share decision making and power in spite of formal centralization. A central question in a federal system is not just how governmental powers and responsibilities are formally divided, but how they are shared, controlled, and influenced after they are divided.

The role of the Interstate Conference in the employment security system suggests that supplementary relationships may further federal-state coordination, integration, cooperation, and unified operation. Integration and coordination may be benefited through these auxiliary federal-state contacts while some of the advantages of a decentralized federal system may be retained. At the minimum, the additional communication in these auxiliary relationships creates some cooperation; at the maximum, decisions are made cooperatively and activities are coordinated.

Cooperation as Power

While many talk in terms of cooperative federalism, cooperation as a term does not define a process but is merely a vague description or prescription about the operation of that process. There is a world of difference, for example, in the definitions of cooperation as harmony, communicating, consulting, and power sharing. Some difficulties and misunderstandings in intergovernmental relationships may be traced to various definitions of cooperation. Although two intergovernmental units may accept cooperation as desirable, both may be dissatisfied with the relationship and feel that the other is not fair in its dealings or living up to its commitments. A federal unit may feel that cooperation is listening to state positions, while the state unit may feel that it entails some degree of state participation and impact; or a state unit may only intend harmonious relationships in its obeisance to cooperation, while the federal unit expects some degree of power sharing.

This employment security study suggests that a useful and meaningful definition of cooperation may be centered around the concept of power. It is a particularly useful focus since power is highly fragmented in the federal as well as in the political system and does not fully correspond to its formal distribution in theory. It also gives some meaning or purpose to the process of cooperation: harmony or consultation without some potential or actual impact is meaningless.

Although it may be useful politically to avoid a rigorous discussion of cooperation, practitioners and scholars are fooling themselves if they ignore this perspective. The abstract concept of cooperative federalism in employment security is accepted by most decision makers, but it should be recognized that this concept has important implications. State cooperation without impact is meaningless.

CHAPTER VI
FOOTNOTES

[1] U.S. Department of Labor, Federal Advisory Council on Employment Security, Committee on Bureau Relations with the Interstate Conference, Report (October 3-4, 1956).

[2] Francis E. Rourke, Intergovernmental Relations in Employment Security (Minneapolis: University of Minnesota Press, 1962) p. 113.

[3] See Chester I. Barnard, The Functions of the Executive (Cambridge: Harvard University Press, 1938) pp. 92-94; and Herbert Simon, Victor A. Thompson, and Donald Smithburg, Public Administration (New York: Alfred A. Knopf, 1950) pp. 180-201.

[4] More specifically, a large group of state officials responded that ICESA goals and purposes were to provide the best employment security program, increase efficiency and effectiveness especially at the state level, improve program design through state action, upgrade administration, improve financing, and improve legislative mandates.

[5] See, for example, William Anderson, Intergovernmental Relations in Review (Minneapolis: University of Minnesota Press, 1960) pp. 130-44; and W. Brooke Graves, American Intergovernmental Relations: Their Origins, Historical Development, and Current Status (New York: Scribner's, 1964)

pp. 783-816. For states' rights viewpoints, see James Jackson Kilpatrick, "The Case for States' Rights," A Nation of States; Essays on the American Federal System, ed. Robert A. Goldwin (Chicago: Rand McNally, 1961) pp. 88-105.

[6] Leonard D. White, The States and the Nation (Baton Rouge: Louisiana State University Press, 1953) p. 3, notes: "If present trends continue for another quarter century, the states may be left hollow shells, operating primarily as the field districts of federal departments and dependent upon the federal treasury for their support."

[7] See Lane Dwinell, "States and the American Federal System," State Government, Vol. 31 (April, 1958) p. 66. George C. S. Benson, "Trends in Intergovernmental Relations," Annals, Vol. 359 (May, 1965) p. 4.

[8] See, for example, William Anderson, The Nation and the States, Rivals or Partners (Minneapolis: University of Minnesota Press, 1955) pp. 141-43; Morton Grodzins, "The Federal System," American Federalism in Perspective, ed. Aaron Wildavsky (Boston: Little, Brown, and Company, 1963) pp. 256-77; and Council of State Governments, Federal Grants-in-Aid (Chicago: Council of State Governments, 1948).

[9] The sixteenth General Assembly of the States, for example, called on the states to assert themselves and redress the power balance. They proposed to amend the Constitution to stop the "drift towards federal domination." "Amending the Constitution to Strengthen the States in the Federal System," State Government, Vol. 36 (Winter, 1963) pp. 10-11.

Bibliography

Although much has been written about the employment security system and unemployment insurance and employment service activities, there are few extensive studies of either the intergovernmental relationship or the Interstate Conference of Employment Security Agencies. The following bibliography includes historical and current sources useful to the student of the ICESA and federalism in employment security.

Books and Monographs

Altmeyer, Arthur J. The Formative Years of Social Security. Madison: University of Wisconsin Press, 1966.

Anderson, William. Intergovernmental Relations in Review. Minneapolis: University of Minnesota Press, 1960.

Atkinson, Raymond C. *The Federal Role in Unemployment Compensation Administration.* Washington, D.C.: Social Science Research Council, 1941.

Becker, Joseph M. *Shared Government in Employment Security; A Study of Advisory Councils.* New York: Columbia University Press, 1959.

Benson, George C. S. *The New Centralization; A Study of Intergovernmental Relationships in the United States.* New York: Farrar and Rinehart, 1941.

Blau, Peter M. *The Dynamics of Bureaucracy; A Study of Interpersonal Relations in Two Government Agencies.* Chicago: University of Chicago Press, 1955.

Clark, Jane Perry. *The Rise of a New Federalism: Federal-State Cooperation in the United States.* New York: Columbia University Press, 1938.

Cohen, Harry. *The Demonics of Bureaucracy: Problems of Change in a Government Agency.* Ames, Iowa: Iowa State University Press, 1965.

Council of State Governments. *The Book of the States*, particularly sections on "Employment Security Administration in the States" and "Significant Developments in Federal-State Relations." Chicago, Illinois: Council of State Governments, biennial, 1935-71.

Elazar, Daniel J. *American Federalism: A View from the States.* New York: Thomas Y. Crowell, 1966.

Graves, W. Brooke. *American Intergovernmental Relations: Their Origins, Historical Development, and Current Status.* New York: Scribners, 1964.

_____. Intergovernmental Relations; An Annotated Chronology of Significant Events, Developments, and Publication with Particular Reference to the Period of the Last Fifty Years. Chicago: Council of State Governments, 1958.

Gray, Herman. Should State Unemployment Insurance be Federalized? New York: American Enterprise Association, 1946.

Grodzins, Norton. The American System; A New View of Government in the United States. Daniel J. Elazar (ed.). Chicago: Rand McNally, 1966.

Haber, William, and Kruger, Daniel H. The Role of the United States Employment Service in a Changing Economy. Kalamazoo, Michigan: W. E. Upjohn Institute, 1964.

Haber, William, and Murray, Merrill G. Unemployment Insurance in the American Economy: An Historical Review and Analysis. Homewood, Illinois: Irwin, 1966.

Key, V. O., Jr. The Administration of Federal Grants to States. Chicago: Public Administration Service, 1937.

Lampman, Robert J. (ed.). Social Security Perspectives. Madison: University of Wisconsin Press, 1962.

Lawyers' Committee for Civil Rights Under Law and National Urban Coalition. Falling Down on the Job: The United States Employment Service and the Disadvantaged. National Urban Coalition and Lawyers' Committee for Civil Rights Under Law, June, 1971.

Rourke, Francis E. *Intergovernmental Relations in Employment Security*. Minneapolis: University of Minnesota Press, 1952.

Selznick, Philip. *TVA and the Grass Roots; A Study in the Sociology of Formal Organization*. New York: Harper and Row, 1966.

Weidner, Edward W. *Intergovernmental Relations As Seen by Public Officials*. Minneapolis: University of Minnesota Press, 1960.

Wildavsky, Aaron (ed.). *American Federalism in Perspective*. Boston: Little, Brown and Co., 1967.

Witte, Edwin E. *The Development of the Social Security Act*. Madison: University of Wisconsin Press, 1962.

Articles and Periodicals

Adrian, Charles R. "State and Local Government Participation in the Design and Administration of Intergovernmental Programs," *Annals*, Vol. 359 (May, 1965) pp. 35-43.

Anderson, Totton J. "Pressure Groups and Intergovernmental Relations," *Annals*, Vol. 359 (May, 1965) pp. 116-26.

Croxton, Fred C. "The Interstate Conference of Employment Security Agencies," *Employment Security Review*, Vol. 7 (December, 1940) pp. 14-16.

Durham, G. Homer. "Politics and Administration in Intergovernmental Relations," *Annals*, Vol. 207 (January, 1940) pp. 1-6.

Elazar, Daniel J. "The Shaping of Intergovernmental Relations in the Twentieth Century," *Annals*, Vol. 359 (May, 1965) pp. 10-22.

Herling, John. "Aborting Federalism" *Washington Daily News*, July 26, 1966, p. 23.

"Interstate Conference of Employment Security Agencies," *Encyclopedia of Associations*. Vol. I: *National Associations of the United States*. Detroit: Gale Research Co., 1964, p. 323.

"Interstate Relations: The Council of State Governments," *The Book of the States*.

"A Job on the Jobless," *I.U.D. Digest* (Industrial Union Department, AFL-CIO), Vol. 3 (Summer, 1958) pp. 10-19.

Key, V. O., Jr. "State Administration of the Social Security Act," *Annals*, Vol. 202 (March, 1939) pp. 153-58.

March, James G. "An Introduction to the Theory and Measurement of Influence," *American Political Science Review*, Vol. 49 (June, 1955) pp. 431-51.

McCulloch, Robert W. "Intergovernmental Relations as Seen by Public Officials," *Annals*, Vol. 359 (May, 1965) pp. 127-36.

Tannenbaum, Arnold S. "The Concept of Organizational Control," *The Journal of Social Issues*, Vol. 12, No. 2 (1956) pp. 50-60.

_____. "Control and Effectiveness in a Voluntary Organization," *American Journal of Sociology*, Vol. 67 (July, 1961), pp. 33-46.

_____. "Control in Organizations: Individual Adjustment and Organizational Performance," *Administrative Science Quarterly*, Vol. 7 (September, 1962), pp. 236-257.

Weidner, Edward W. "Decision-Making in a Federal System," *American Federalism in Perspective*. Aaron Wildavsky (ed.). Boston: Little, Brown, and Co., pp. 229-56.

_____. "Secretary's Order No. 20-67; Subject: Policy responsibility, and procedures for consultation with heads of State and local governments in development of Federal rules, standards, procedures, and guidelines." September 13, 1967.

_____. "Secretary's Order No. 14-69; Subject: Reorganization of the Manpower Administration and Delegation of Authority and Assignment of Responsibilities for Manpower Programs." March 14, 1969.

U.S. Department of Labor, Bureau of Employment Security. Historical Statistics of Employment Security Activities, 1938-66. January, 1968.

U.S. House of Representatives, Committee on Appropriations. Department of Labor, and Health, Education, and Welfare, and Related Agencies Appropriation Bill. Particularly 89th Congress, 1st Session, April 29, 1965; 89th Congress, 2nd Session, 1966; and 90th Congress, 2nd Session, 1968.

U.S. House of Representatives, Committee on Government Operations. Federal-State-Local Relations: Federal Departments and Agencies. 85th Congress, 2nd Session, April, 1958.

_____. Replies from State and Local Governments to Questionaire on Intergovernmental Relations. 85th Congress, 1st Session, June 17, 1957.

_____. Staff Report on Replies from Federal Agencies to Questionaire on Intergovernmental Relations. 84th Congress, 2nd Session, August, 1956.

U.S. Joint Federal-State Action Committee. Final Report of the Joint Federal-State Action Committee to the President of the United States and to the Chairman of the Governor's Conference. 1960.

Public Documents

U.S. Advisory Commission on Intergovernmental Relations. <u>The Advisory Commission on Intergovernmental Relations; To Improve the Effectiveness of the American Federal System Through Increased Cooperation among National, State and Local Levels of Government</u>. November, 1962.

U.S. Bureau of the Budget. "Circular No. A-85: Consultation with heads of State and local governments in development of Federal rules, regulations, standards, procedures and guidelines." June 28, 1967.

U.S. Commission on Intergovernmental Relations. <u>A Description of Twenty-Five Federal Grant-In-Aid Programs</u>. June, 1955.

_____. <u>A Report to the President for Transmittal to the Congress</u>. June, 1955.

_____. <u>A Study Committee Report on Unemployment Compensation and Employment Service</u>. June, 1955.

_____. <u>Summaries of Survey Reports on the Administrative and Fiscal Impact of Grants-In-Aid</u>. June, 1955.

U.S. Commission on Organization of the Executive Branch of the Government. <u>Federal-State-Relations by the Council of State Governments</u>. Senate Document, 81st Congress, 1st Session, March 25, 1949.

U.S. Department of Labor. <u>Organization Manual</u>.

_____. "Secretary's Memorandum: Manpower Administration." December 19, 1967.

U.S. President. <u>Manpower Report of the President including A Report on Manpower Requirements, Resources, Utilization, and Training by the United States Department of Labor</u>. Annual.

_____. "Memorandum to Heads of Certain Federal Agencies: Advice and Consultation with State and Local Officials." November 11, 1966.

U.S. Senate, Committee on Government Operations, Subcommittee on Intergovernmental Relations. <u>Intergovernmental Relations</u>. 88th Congress, 1st Session, April 1, 1963.

_____. <u>Creative Federalism</u>. 89th Congress, 2nd Session, 1966.

_____. <u>Creative Federalism</u>. 90th Congress, 1st Session, 1967.

_____. <u>The Federal System as Seen by State and Local Officials; Results of a Questionaire Dealing with Intergovernmental Relations</u>. 88th Congress, 1st Session, 1963.

_____. <u>Intergovernmental Cooperation Act of 1967 and Related Legislation</u>. 90th Congress, 2nd Session, 1968.

ICESA Documents

Interstate Conference of Employment Security Agencies. <u>Constitution and Code</u>.

_____. <u>Guide to Authority and Responsibilities of the Interstate Benefit Payments Committee</u>.

_____. <u>Minutes of the National Executive Committee Meetings</u>. 1955-71.

_____. <u>Proceedings of the Annual Meeting</u>. 1940-70.

Interstate Conference of Unemployment Compensation Agencies. <u>Annual Meeting</u>. 1937-39.

Unpublished Material

Federal Advisory Council, Committee on Bureau Relations with Interstate Conference. "Report," October 3-4, 1956.

Williams, David G. <u>Cooperative Intergovernmental Relationships: The Interstate Conference of Employment Security Agencies</u>. Unpublished Ph.D. dissertation, Graduate School of Public Affairs, State University of New York at Albany, 1970.